TIME
LIFE
BOOKS

This volume is part of a series offering home
owners detailed instructions on repairs,
construction and improvements which they can
undertake themselves.

HOME REPAIR
AND IMPROVEMENT

BUILT-INS

BY THE EDITORS OF
TIME-LIFE BOOKS

TIME-LIFE BOOKS
AMSTERDAM

TIME-LIFE BOOKS
EUROPEAN EDITOR: Kit van Tulleken
Assistant European Editor: Gillian Moore
Design Director: Ed Skyner
Photography Director: Pamela Marke
Chief of Research: Vanessa Kramer
Chief Sub-Editor: Ilse Gray

HOME REPAIR AND IMPROVEMENT
EDITORIAL STAFF FOR BUILT-INS
Editor: William Frankel
Assistant Editor: David Thiemann
Designer: Kenneth E. Hancock
Picture Editor: Adrian Allen
Associate Designer: Lorraine D. Rivard
Text Editors: Bonnie Bohling Kreitler, Leslie Marshall,
Lydia Preston, Brooke Stoddard
Staff Writers: Lynn R. Addison, William C. Banks,
Megan Barnett, Robert A. Doyle, Malachy Duffy,
Steven J. Forbis, Peter Pocock, William Worsley
Chief Researcher: Phyllis K. Wise
Art Associates: George Bell, Daniel J. McSweeney,
Richard Whiting
Editorial Assistant: Susanne S. Trice

EUROPEAN EDITION
Series Director: Jackie Matthews
Designer: Paul Reeves
Writer-Researcher: Susie Bicknell
Sub-Editors: Frances Dixon, Hilary Hockman

EDITORIAL PRODUCTION
Chief: Jane Hawker
Production Assistant: Maureen Kelly
Editorial Department: Theresa John, Debra Lelliott

THE CONSULTANTS: Leslie Stokes was a self-employed carpenter and joiner
for seven years, specializing in purpose-made joinery and internal
fittings. Since 1976 he has taught in the building department at the
Hammersmith and West London College.

After studying architecture at the Boston Architectural Center,
Lawrence R. England Jr. began his association with L. R. England and
Sons, a family custom cabinet-making and wood-carving business started
by his grandfather in 1900.

Robert L. Petersen has been a cabinet-maker in Maryland and Virginia
since 1971. His own particular speciality is 18th century Palladian
design and architecture.

Yves A. Fedrigault began working as a cabinet-maker at the age of 16 in
Bordeaux, France. He moved to the United States in 1963, and in 1965 he
started his own business, Y. A. F. Development, Inc., which specializes in
custom-made built-ins and the restoration and remodelling of old houses.

Roswell W. Ard is a consulting structural engineer and a professional
home inspector in northern Michigan. He has written professional papers
on wood-frame construction techniques.

Contents

1

Cabinets Plain and Fancy

To most people, the word "built-in" stands for two basic elements in a modern house—kitchen cabinets and living-room bookcases. In fact, the convenience of built-ins has spread throughout the house, in room dividers and storage walls; in benches, couches and tables; and in beds that fold into the walls. Some built-ins, such as a sewing centre or an indoor garden, create new, special-purpose living and work areas.

Whatever the location or use, a built-in is inexpensive, costing much less than its factory-made equivalent. It fits a particular room and particular needs, without wasted space or an awkward arrangement of doors or drawers. And its workmanship is suited to its surroundings—a simple backless bookcase for a child's bedroom, perhaps, or a fine hardwood veneered cabinet for a dining room.

Solid timber can serve for simple built-ins such as shelves, open bookcases *(opposite)* and small drawers; it is easy to cut and finish, and inexpensive softwoods such as pine usually come in widths up to 225 mm, and sometimes even wider. However, fine woods are prohibitively expensive in pieces even that wide, and most built-ins require wood that is wider still. As a result the common materials for built-ins are plywood, blockboard, fibreboard or chipboard—all cheaper than solid timber.

To a woodworker, these manufactured boards have great advantages. They come in unblemished sheets with straight edges and a uniform thickness, and each part of a built-in can be made from a single section. They do not warp or twist, and seldom split or crack.

The type of plywood most commonly used for built-ins has hardwood face veneers and inner plies of less expensive softwood. Blockboard consists of strips of softwood or hardwood sandwiched between single or treble hardwood veneers. Medium-density fibreboard is often substituted for blockboard; it is very stable and gives a superb finish when painted, but it must be cut on a machine, which creates a lot of dust. Chipboard, cheaper and more suitable than either plywood or blockboard for fixing plastic laminate to, is also available with hardwood or melamine surfaces, but should not be used in rooms subject to damp.

Birch veneer is best for surfaces to be painted or stained. Birch grain is not particularly attractive, however; if a clear finish is to be applied, more expensive woods, such as elm, mahogany and oak, are generally preferred. The veneered sides of manufactured boards are graded according to quality. Use grades A or B, which have unblemished surfaces, for a clear or stained finish. Some boards, known as "good one side", have a high grade veneer on one side only; other boards may have the same grade of veneer on both sides.

Finally, for any part of a built-in requiring solid timber, it is important to remember that the dimensions of prepared (planed-all-round) timber are usually 5 or 6 mm smaller than the original, or nominal, size from which it was produced and by which it is sold. Always check the actual dimensions of any piece of timber before starting work. In this book nominal timber measurements are used only.

Open Shelving: Units for Walls, Alcoves and Corners

The simplest of all built-ins is a set of open shelves fixed to the wall. Such shelving can be constructed using plain butt joints; the individual pieces can be nailed or screwed directly to the wall *(pages 11–12)*, or fitted together with jointing blocks and then attached to the wall *(here and overleaf)*.

As they are assembled on site, these units are easier to install than a cabinet made in a workshop *(pages 16–19)* which has to be transported to its final position, risking damage. Yet, properly built, they fill a variety of uses from displaying china to creating an informal bookcase.

Shelf units are usually rectangular and can be placed along a wall, in a corner or in an alcove. Some are triangular to fit neatly into a corner, providing shelving suitable for storage or display. Support can be either permanent using jointing blocks, or adjustable using metal standards with movable clips *(page 11, above)*.

The dimensions of shelving units are determined by the room and the purpose. If they run from floor to ceiling, the side pieces can rise to the ceiling, or stop 300 mm short; the gap can be covered with a fascia and coving *(pages 50–51)*. The length of the unit is variable but the possible span of a single shelf depends on the thickness of the material being used and the weight the shelf is to support. Generally, the following spans should not be exceeded: 500 mm for 9 mm-thick material, 600 mm for 12 mm, 700 mm for 15 mm and 800 mm for 18 mm. If you are planning to store heavy items such as tightly packed books and records, or piles of crockery, either shorten the span or divide it with partition shelf supports *(page 114)*.

The depth of shelves will also vary according to the items they will carry: paperbacks and most hardback books need a depth of 150 to 175 mm; large books need 175 to 300 mm; records require a depth of 320 mm; stereo equipment needs 450 mm or more and a television at least 600 mm.

Timber or any of the manufactured boards may be used to make the shelf units. If using blockboard, make certain the core runs along the length of the shelf. Melamine-covered chipboard is a popular choice, as no additional finish is required, and standard 1800 by 300 by 15 mm panels will make up an average-sized shelf unit with the minimum of cutting *(below and opposite)*. Other manufactured boards and timber will need a surface finish *(pages 42–43)* and the exposed edges must be concealed with iron-on tape, glued edging strips, or pinned and glued 18 by 18 mm lipping. Jointing blocks, designed to fasten to the faces of chipboard instead of into its crumbly end grain, may be used to join any of the manufactured boards.

Before starting work, remove the skirting board from the wall where the shelving will be fixed. Insert the end of a crowbar behind the skirting board at one corner and, using a block of wood placed between the bar and the wall as a fulcrum, level the skirting board away from the wall. Keep the board out from the wall with a small wedge of wood as you move the bar along the wall in 400 mm steps. The skirting board can be used to trim any wall space on either side of the unit once it is installed. Where you cannot remove the skirting board easily—if, for instance, it is caught behind layers of flooring—mark and cut the base of the unit to fit round it.

If you are fitting shelving into an alcove, check the walls for squareness before you begin work. Measure the distance between the side walls at two points—where the front and back of the unit will lie—then construct the unit to fit the shortest distance; if the alcove is narrower at the back than at the front, you can fill the gap with a piece of wood cut to fit.

Rectangular Shelving Along a Wall

1 **Making the base.** Cut back and front pieces for the base to the length of the unit from timber 25 mm thick and the same height as the skirting board. Cut side pieces for the base 100 mm shorter than the planned depth of the shelf unit. Set the pieces on edge in a rectangle, the side pieces between the front and the back, and nail 75 mm lost-head nails through each long piece into the ends of the short ones. Place the base against the wall and drive 75 mm lost-head nails at an angle through the back piece into the floor at 150 mm intervals; for a concrete floor, fix the base with masonry nails.

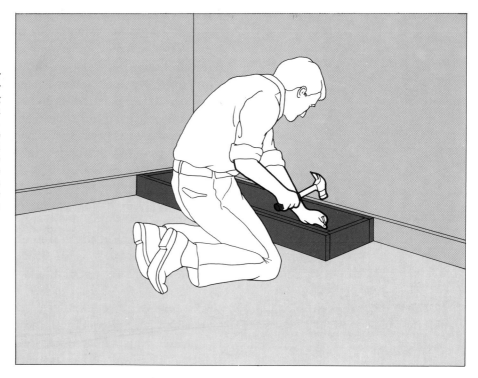

2 **Marking up the side pieces.** From a standard 1800 by 300 by 15 mm chipboard panel, cut two side pieces to the height of the shelf unit less 85 mm. Using a steel square, draw a line across both side pieces to mark the position of the bottom edge of the centre shelf. Then mark points 25 mm in from both sides of each side piece, and 15 mm up from the bottom. Join these points together using a straightedge and a pencil.

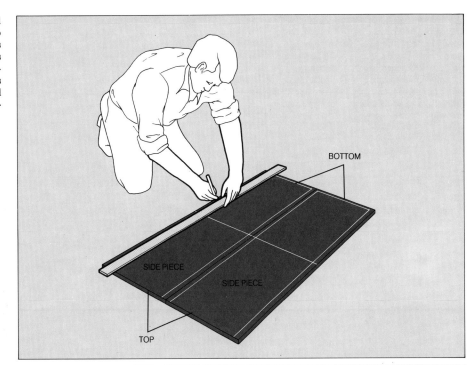

BOTTOM

SIDE PIECE

SIDE PIECE

TOP

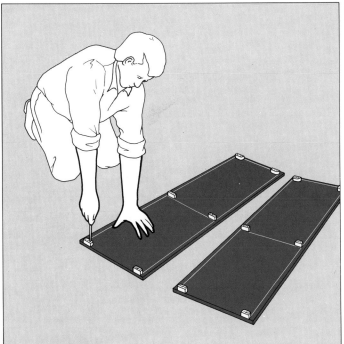

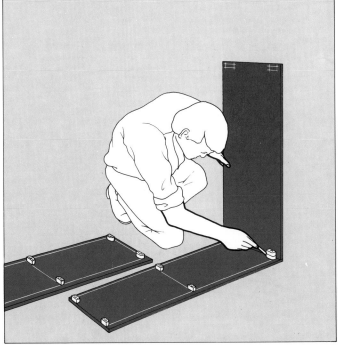

3 **Fixing the jointing block bases.** Separate the bases from the tops of 12 jointing blocks by removing the central screw. Working on one side piece, lay two bases against the shelf line and another two inside the bottom line—the flat side of each block base should lie against the pencil line. All the bases should be just within the 25 mm lines. Place two more bases flush with the top edge of the side piece. Position the remaining 6 jointing block bases in the same pattern on the other side piece. Use a bradawl to start two screwholes through each base (*above*), then fix the bases to the side pieces with the screws provided.

4 **Fixing block tops.** Cut a top for the unit the same length as the overall length of the unit, and a shelf and bottom 30 mm shorter. Set the bottom on a side piece against the two lower block bases; place a block top on each base and outline them in pencil on the bottom. Turn the bottom piece through 180 degrees so that its other short edge rests on the short edge of the side piece and again outline block tops on the bottom piece (*above*). With the bottom on the floor, screw the block tops in position inside each outline. Repeat for the centre shelf. For the top, place the edge on the floor flush against the top edge of the side piece.

9

5 **Assembling the unit.** Position the bottom on one of the side pieces so that the jointing blocks pair up and secure the block parts with the long central screw. Fix the centre shelf in the same way *(right)*. Place one edge of the top on the floor against thé free end of the side piece, so the jointing blocks pair up; screw them together. Turn the semi-completed unit over, placing it on to the second side piece. Align and secure the paired blocks as before *(right, below)*.

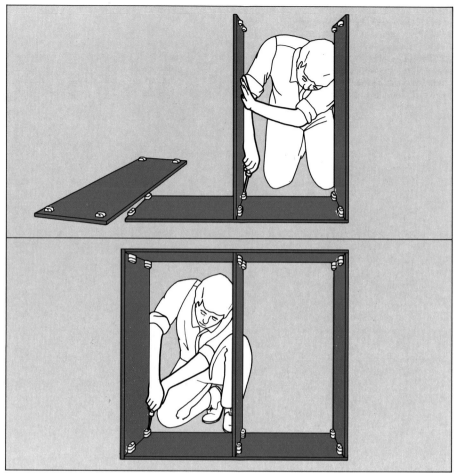

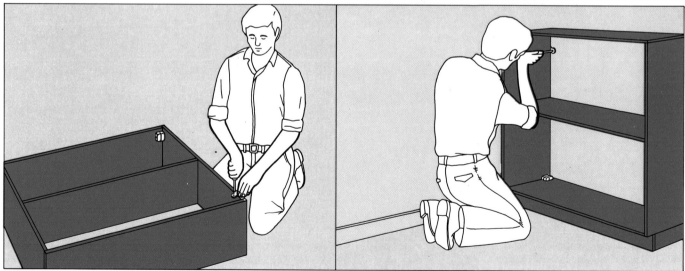

6 **Fixing the unit to the wall.** Secure a mirror plate to the back edge of each side piece 50 mm down from the top *(above, left)* using chipboard screws. (If you are not making the unit in chipboard, use 16 mm No. 4 wood screws.) Place the unit upright on its base and mark the wall through the mirror plate fixing holes. Remove the unit, drill and plug pilot holes, and secure the shelf unit to the wall with 37 mm No. 6 screws *(above, right)*. To secure the unit to its base, nail 37 mm panel pins through the bottom of the unit and into the back piece of the base at 300 mm intervals.

Standards for Adjustable Shelving

Where adjustable shelving is required, a system of movable clips that slot into vertical metal standards can be used to support the shelves instead of the jointing blocks (*page 9 and opposite*) and cleats (*page 101*) normally used for supporting fixed shelving. The standards may be either surface-mounted, leaving a 5 mm gap at the end of each shelf, or set into a vertical groove cut before the shelf unit is assembled (*pages 22–25*). Install the standards in pairs about 25 mm from the back and front of each side piece, using screws in pre-drilled holes.

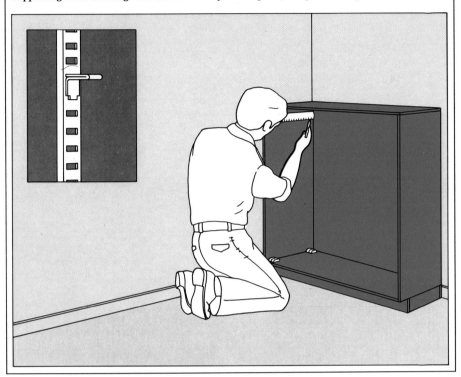

Triangular Shelves to Fit into a Corner

1 **Making a template.** From an 18 mm-thick piece of manufactured board, cut a square with sides 20 mm longer than the planned shelf sides. Offer the square to the corner to check that it fits neatly. If it does not fit because the walls are not square, plane the edges until they lie flush with the walls. Then, starting from the corner of the board that was fitted to the wall, measure and mark the length of the planned shelf sides along the two adjacent edges. Using a pencil and a straightedge, join these marks together to indicate the front of the shelf unit; draw a parallel line 75 mm closer to the corner to mark the position of the front of the base.

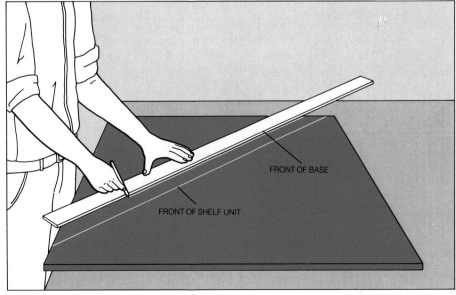

FRONT OF BASE

FRONT OF SHELF UNIT

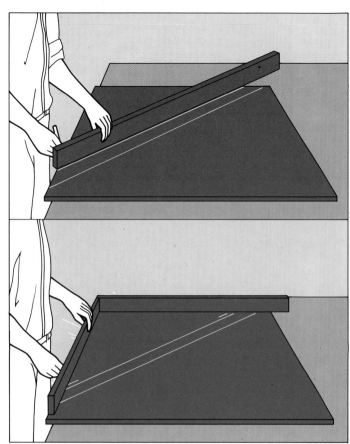

2 **Making the base.** To make the base front, set a piece of timber 25 mm thick and the same height as the skirting board, on edge against the line marked for the base front. Mark a short line at each side of the template where the piece of timber meets the edges. Also mark the position of each edge of the template on both the front and back of the timber piece *(left, above)*. Cut the base front by making an angled 45-degree cut between each pair of marks.

To make the base sides, place a piece of timber 25 mm thick and the same height as the skirting board along one side of the template with one end on the corner. At the other end, mark on the back and front of the timber the point where it crosses the base front marked lines. Butt a second 25 mm piece of timber against the first *(left, below)*, and mark it in the same way. Cut pieces of timber at 45-degree angles between these marks. Fasten the base sides to the walls with masonry nails, then secure the base front to the sides, using lost-head nails.

3 **Fitting the bottom and sides.** Cut the template along the front line to form the bottom of the unit; fix this to the base with 37 mm lost-head nails every 150 mm. Transfer the measurement of one side of the bottom to a piece of board cross-cut to the desired height of the unit, then cut the piece lengthwise along the proposed front edge with a bevel cut to match the angle of the base, using a circular saw. Fasten the side piece to the wall with plugged 50 mm No. 8 screws or 40 mm masonry nails at 300 mm intervals down the front edge of the side piece *(below)*.

Measure the other side of the bottom from the side piece to the outer edge, and cut and fasten the second side piece.

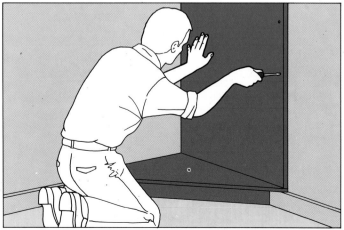

4 **Completing the unit.** Set the remaining section of the template on top of the side pieces; plane it down if necessary *(Step 1)*. Replace the top and mark the position of the front edges of the side pieces on to the underside of the top; join these two points using a straightedge. Cut the top along this line and nail it to the sides. To make a shelf, hold a rectangular piece of board inside the unit and mark where its sides meet the front edge of each side piece *(above)*. Cut along a line drawn 5 mm inside these marks so the shelf will be slightly inset.

Repeat for each shelf required, installing jointing blocks or standards as shelf supports.

A Table Saw for Precise Cuts and Joints

A circular saw with jigs and guides (*page 20*) is adequate for most built-ins, but the tool preferred by professionals is the table saw. The blade of a table saw protrudes through a slot in a perfectly flat metal table. For cuts with the grain, an adjustable rip fence clamps on to the table parallel to the blade; for crosscuts and angle cuts, an adjustable mitre gauge is used.

A 250 mm table saw has a blade of the same diameter and will cut through a board 75 to 87 mm thick. The rip capacity, measured between the rip fence and the side of the blade, ideally should be at least 600 mm, so that the saw can cut along the centre of a 2440 by 1220 mm board; on some models this cut may require an outrigger table. A delivery top may also be necessary at the back of the table to support large boards as they are being pushed through. The ideal distance between the back of the blade and the table edge is 1200 mm. Also, there should be at least 300 mm between the front of the table and the edge of the blade, to accommodate a 300 by 25 mm board for a crosscut.

The synthetic resin glue binding manufactured boards quickly blunts ordinary steel blades, so it is well worth investing in a tungsten carbide-tipped blade if you do much sawing. A fine-toothed crosscut blade reduces chipping and splintering: the more teeth on a blade, the better the finish.

The blade of a table saw rotates towards the operator. To reduce the risk of injury, the blade is covered with a guard, and a riving knife, placed 12 mm or less behind the blade, prevents a board from binding or kicking back as well as stopping a helper from accidentally touching the rear of the blade. If binding and kickbacks occur frequently, get your blade professionally adjusted, and check that the riving knife is one or two gauges thicker than the blade.

To prevent splintering of surfaces that will show in the completed job, always saw boards with the hidden side down—the bottom surface chips more than the top. On melamine-faced chipboard, stick masking tape over the cutting line to reduce splintering. In addition, feed boards into the blade slowly; a fast feed makes rough cuts.

Anatomy of a table saw. The blade of this saw protrudes through a slot in the tabletop and is covered by a pivoting guard that slides over a board as it is cut. Placed directly behind and in the same slot as the blade, a riving knife separates the two sides of the board after it has been cut. The blade height is adjusted by a crank beneath the table, the blade tilt by a knurled handwheel behind the crank.

The mitre gauge, used to guide crosscuts and angle cuts, usually slides in the groove on the left hand side of the blade, but can also be used in a right-hand groove. The gauge has stops at 90 degrees and 45 degrees, and can be locked at other angles with a knob. A home-made wooden extension is screwed to the face of the gauge to keep long boards from wobbling as they are cut. The rip fence slides on guide bars at the front and back of the table and can be locked at any position on the guide bars.

For rip cuts on boards under 1½ metres long, a wooden face is fastened to the inside of the rip fence level with the front of the blade. This auxiliary fence prevents the board binding between the blade and the rip fence after it has been cut, as well as preventing panels less than 6 mm thick from slipping under the regular fence. For rip cuts, grooves and housings made on the edges or ends of boards, a tall wooden fence is used for additional support.

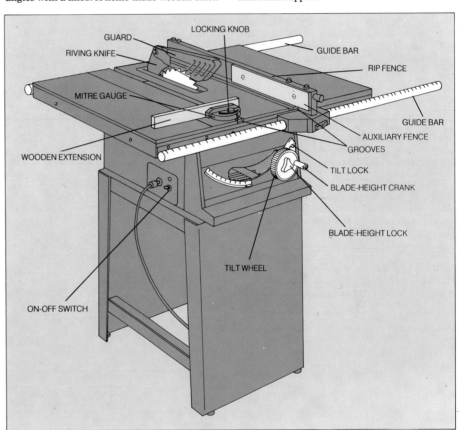

Safety Tips for Table Saws

In addition to the common-sense rules that apply to the use of all power tools—wear goggles and comfortable but not loose clothes—special precautions are required for a table saw:

☐ Adjust the saw before you turn it on, never while it is running.

☐ Before cutting knotty boards, knock large or loose knots out with a hammer.

☐ Never saw boards freehand; always use a rip fence or a mitre gauge.

☐ If the blade stalls, turn the saw off immediately; do not try to free a stalled blade while the motor is on.

☐ Do not touch waste pieces less than 300 mm long before the blade stops.

☐ Never reach over or behind the blade—a sudden kickback could yank your hand into the blade.

☐ Always keep your hands far away from the blade, using a push stick as needed to guide the work.

Setting Up for the Basic Cuts

Crosscutting. Set the mitre gauge at 90 degrees, place the edge of the board against the gauge and set the blade so its top is about 3 mm above the board. Align the marked cutting line with the blade and turn the saw on, then hold the board firmly against the mitre gauge with your left hand and push the gauge forwards with your right, moving the board into the blade. Caution: keep both hands on the same side of the blade; otherwise, the board will kick back. When the board is about 50 mm beyond the blade, slide it slightly to the left and pull the mitre gauge back.

To cut several pieces to the same length, clamp a wooden stop block to the table next to the rip fence at the front of the saw *(inset)*, slide the board sideways to the stop, then make the cut in the normal way. Never use the rip fence as a stop block, because the board could bind between the fence and the blade.

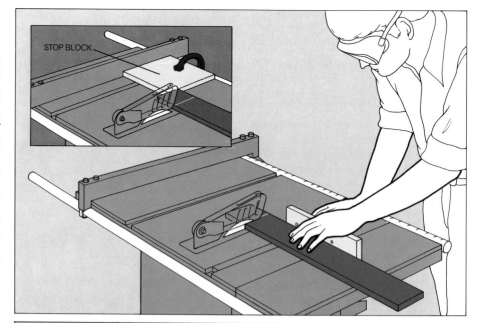

STOP BLOCK

Cutting down the board. Fasten an auxiliary fence to the rip fence so that one end of the auxiliary fence is level with the front of the blade. Set the rip fence for the width of the cut. Position the board against the auxiliary fence and turn the saw on. Hook a 400 mm push stick over the edge of the board between the auxiliary fence and the blade. Slowly move the board into the blade with the push stick, holding the board against the fence with your left hand *(right)*. When your left hand is about 150 mm in front of the guard, pull it away and finish the cut with the push stick. Push the board beyond the blade and guard, then slide it to the side of the fence and pull it back.

To cut narrow pieces, where it would be dangerous to hold the board with your left hand, hook the push stick over the left-hand corner of the board. Move the board through the blade, angling the push stick so that the board is kept against the auxiliary fence *(inset)*.

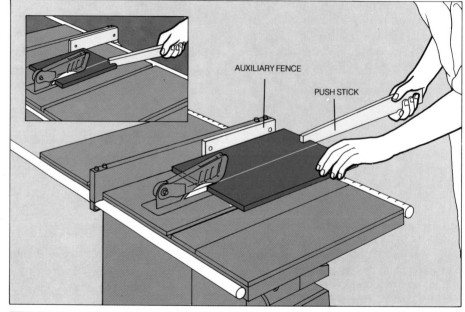

AUXILIARY FENCE

PUSH STICK

Angle cuts. Turn the head of the mitre gauge to the desired angle and tighten the locking knob; the gauge ordinarily is angled towards the blade because it can cut wider boards in this position, but it also can be angled away from the blade. Align the cutting line with the blade, start the saw and push the mitre gauge forwards.

Hold the edge of the board tightly against the face of the gauge with both hands; otherwise the board may creep slightly and spoil the angle of the cut. If creeping persists, run wood screws part way through the mitre-gauge extension; the screw points will keep the wood from sliding.

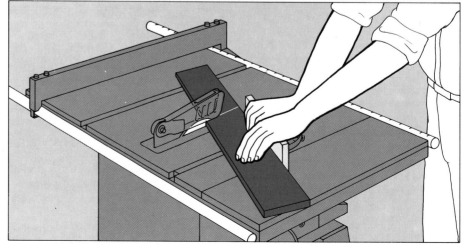

Cutting angles in wide boards. Reverse the mitre gauge in its slot *(right)*, placing the head at the far side of the table. Push the board into the saw blade, holding its far edge against the gauge, until the gauge head reaches the far edge of the table. Then turn off the saw, move the gauge to the usual position, restart the saw and complete the cut *(right, below)*.

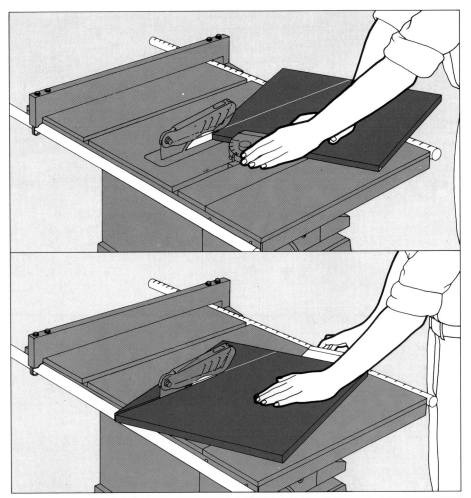

Making bevel cuts. To bevel across the grain, fit the mitre gauge in the slot that the blade tilts away from, and set the gauge at 90 degrees. Adjust the angle of the saw, using the saw's tilt scale or sighting the blade against the angle marked on the board. Hold the board against the gauge very firmly—bevel cuts tend to pull the board sideways—and make the cut in the same way as you would a simple crosscut.

For a compound cut *(left inset)*, set the tilt adjustment and the mitre gauge to the desired angles, then cut as you would for an angle cut.

To make a bevel rip cut *(right inset)*, hold the work tightly against the rip fence and feed it as you would for a rip cut. Bevel rip cuts are best made with the rip fence on the side of the table that the blade tilts away from, if the design of your saw permits this.

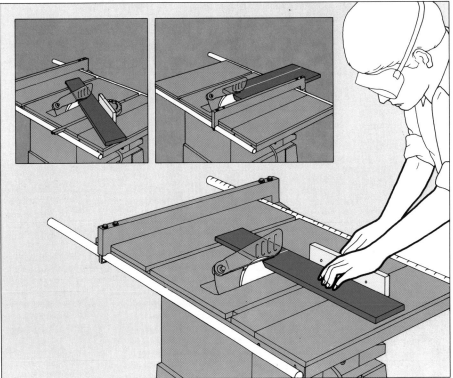

The Professional Way of Building a Cabinet

Most built-in cabinets are made in a home workshop, then fastened to the house, and with good reason—they are better than cabinets assembled in place. In a workshop, you can use the strong, invisible joints typical of fine furniture and the cabinets can be fitted with intricate drawers and panelled doors. If you own a table saw, you naturally build in the shop, but even with portable tools, shop work is easier.

Cabinets are often divided into those that hang from a wall (below) and those that are fastened to the floor (opposite), although both are made in much the same way. Each has a carcass—a box consisting of top, bottom, back, sides and partitions fastened together with glue and nails (pages 26–29). To provide a solid support for the doors, the front of the carcass is fitted with a face frame of solid planed-all-round timber 50 mm wide (pages 30–33).

The design of a cabinet is a matter of individual taste and requirements—doors, drawers and shelves can be arranged in a variety of ways (pages 31–36)—but a few rules of thumb do apply. The base cabinets for a kitchen are usually 900 mm high and no more than 600 mm deep; in other rooms, the depth limitation is generally 450 mm but the height depends on function and is restricted only by the height of the room ceiling. Drawers are generally no more than 600 mm wide, doors no more than 500 mm. Wall-mounted cabinets are generally about 300 mm deep, to allow easy access to the back of the cabinet; most bookcases are 250 to 300 mm deep. To prevent sagging, the length of shelves should not exceed 800 mm; the width depends on their contents.

A cabinet made in a workshop and carried to its final location must be small

Two Basic Cabinets

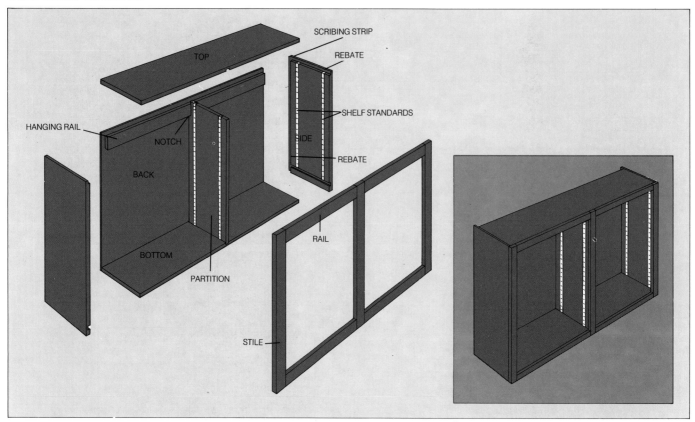

A wall-mounted cabinet. The sides, top, bottom and partition of this typical cabinet are made of 18 mm board. Each side has a rebate, or step cut, 19 mm wide and 6 mm deep along its back edge; another rebate along its top, and a housing, of the same dimensions, cut 28 mm above its bottom. The cabinet top, 24 mm shorter than the overall length of the cabinet and 19 mm narrower than the sides, fits into the rebates at the tops of the sides; the bottom, cut to the same dimensions, fits into the housings near the bottoms of the sides.

The back, made of 6 mm plywood or hardboard, fits into the rebates along the back edges of the sides and extends over the edges of the top and bottom; on each side piece, the 13 mm of rebate protruding beyond the back is a scribing strip (page 48), used to fit the cabinet to the wall when the unit is installed. A hanging rail—a strip of 18 mm board 75 mm wide—runs across the top of the back; it ties the back of the top and sides and serves as a firm brace when the cabinet is fastened to the wall (page 47, Step 3). A centre partition, 19 mm narrower and 52 mm shorter than the side pieces, is notched round the rail and fits into housings in the top and bottom. Standards for shelves fit into grooves in the partition and sides; the partition grooves are offset.

The edges at the front of the cabinet are covered by a face frame of solid timber 19 mm thick and 50 mm wide (pages 30–33), with vertical stiles as long as the sides and horizontal rails fastened between the stiles with loose tongues (pages 30–33) or dowels (page 33, bottom).

enough to fit through the doorways, turn the corners and negotiate the staircases of the house. If the cabinet is too big to be manoeuvred in one piece, or if it is longer than 2400 mm—the length of a sheet of manufactured board—build it in sections (page 18, top) and fit the sections together as you install the unit. It must be possible to tilt a floor-to-ceiling cabinet upright without scraping the ceiling; the length of a diagonal measured between opposite corners on one side should be at least 25 mm less than the ceiling height.

After deciding the overall dimensions of a cabinet, sketch each piece to scale on graph paper, using one grid square for each 10 mm or 20 mm, or more, depending on the size of the grid. On your sketch, mark the width and length of all the pieces and the size and location of cuts such as housings, grooves, rebates and notches (pages 22–25) to be made within a piece.

For a wood finish, group together the pieces that should have the same appearance—sides and shelves which require two good faces, for example, or tops and bottoms which need only one. In addition, make certain that matching pieces will have the grain running the right way: vertically for sides and horizontally for the tops and bottoms. Then make a cutting sketch for each sheet. On this sketch, set pieces of the same width in a row, to be sawn with a single rip cut—allow at least 3 mm between pieces for the saw kerf—and plan the use of offcuts for narrow, hidden parts such as the base, hanging rails and drawer supports.

Make the long rip cuts first, measuring each time for a perfectly straight edge and marking the ends of the cut with a sharp pencil; you need not draw a cutting line as a table-saw fence or circular-saw guide will keep the blade straight. If you use a table saw, cut the pieces of the same width one after another, without moving the fence. For crosscuts, mark and cut the first piece of each length, then set the cut piece on each of the matching pieces and trace round it, to eliminate the errors that creep in with repeated measurements.

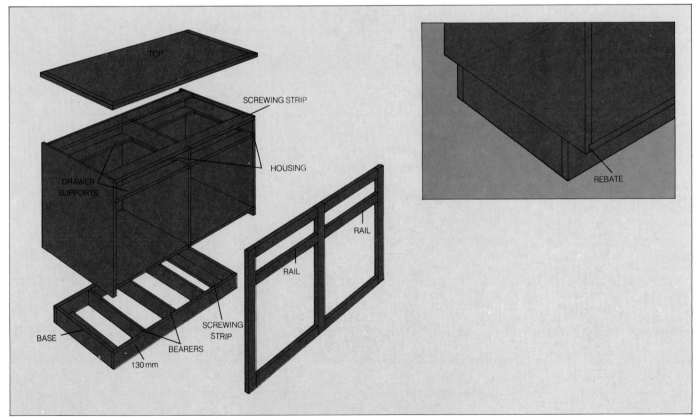

A base cabinet. A cabinet fastened to the floor fits together similarly to a wall-mounted one, but has several additional components. It rests on a base of 18 mm board fastened together with butt joints and reinforced with crosspieces called bearers. The base is 130 mm high and is set back 75 mm from the front frame and from each exposed side of the cabinet, but the frame and side overlap the base by 30 mm, leaving a protective kick space 100 mm high and 75 mm deep. Exposed sides, shown here, are housed like those of a wall-mounted cabinet; a side that fits against a wall or another cabinet is rebated and ends flush with the bottom (inset).

The back is fastened directly to the wall without a hanging rail. The base is fastened to the floor through screwing strips. At the top, two screwing strips of 18 mm board, 100 mm wide, run across the front and back and are housed for a centre partition. The top overhangs the cabinet by 25 mm on each side and is fastened by short screws driven up through the strips.

In a cabinet with drawers, as here, the partition is offset slightly, so one of its sides is flush with an edge of the centre stile; when a drawer is installed, spacers are fastened to the other side of the partition and to the sides of the cabinet (page 36, Step 1). At the bottom of each drawer opening, drawer supports—strips of 18 mm board, 100 mm wide—are set in 6 mm housings in the sides and in the partition at the front and back of the cabinet; additional rails in the face frame conceal the exposed edges of the supports.

Variations of the Basic Cabinets

A floor-to-ceiling bookcase. Elements of wall-mounted and base cabinets—a hanging rail and a base—are combined in this unit, designed to be fastened to both the floor and the top of a wall. A bookcase higher than 1800 mm, like the one illustrated here, is reinforced with fixed shelves that fit into housings 6 mm deep at or near the middle of each side and partition. The top rail of the face frame is 75 mm wide—25 mm wider than the other parts of the frame; when the cabinet is installed *(page 51)*, coving covers 25 mm of this rail, and its exposed width matches that of the other pieces.

A floor-to-ceiling bookcase that is more than 1800 mm wide, like this one, cannot fit through a doorway in one piece; it is actually composed of several sections, each an independent cabinet. The sections rest on a continuous base, with joints in the front and back pieces made between bearers and reinforced by hidden cleats. The cabinet sections are screwed together when the bookcase is installed *(page 49, Step 1)*.

A room divider. Open on both sides, a see-through base cabinet can be built with a worktop that juts out from a wall, as in this example, or it can be built as a ceiling-high partition between two areas. The worktop of a 900 mm cabinet overhangs each side by 25 mm; the top of a floor-to-ceiling cabinet is finished like that of a wall-mounted cabinet *(page 16)*, and a fixed shelf *(above)* is added near the middle of the unit.

A room divider is generally 450 to 600 mm deep, permitting easy access from either face of the unit. Structural rigidity is provided by frames fastened to both faces of the unit, rather than by a single face frame and a conventional back.

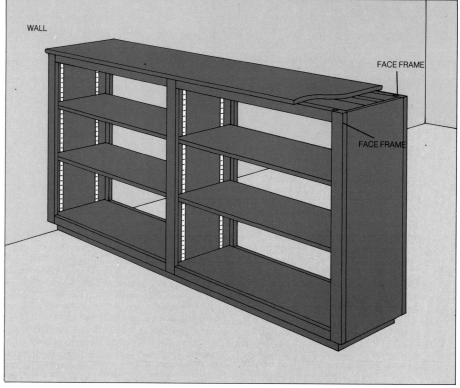

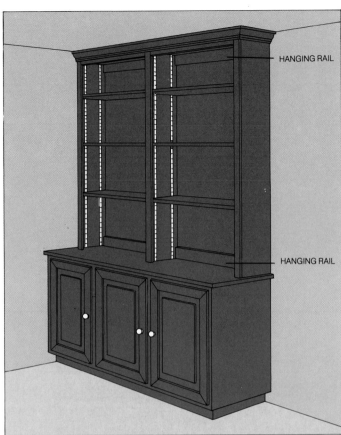

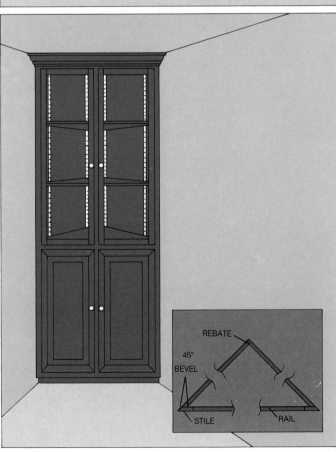

A cabinet and bookcase combined. The cabinet of this unit, generally about 800 mm high and 450 mm deep, is built in the usual way *(page 17)*; the bookcase, generally as wide as the base and about 300 mm deep, resembles a wall-mounted cabinet, but has a second hanging rail at the bottom. The sides of the bookcase bear on those of the cabinet, 25 mm inside the edges of the cabinet top, and the sections are fastened together in the course of installation *(page 49, Step 1)*.

An island cabinet. This kitchen cabinet, usually set beneath an overhead island unit, is generally 900 mm high and 750 to 1000 mm deep. A partition runs from front to back, and an 18 mm false back fits into housings at the middle of the partition, sides and bottom. Face frames are installed on both front and back.

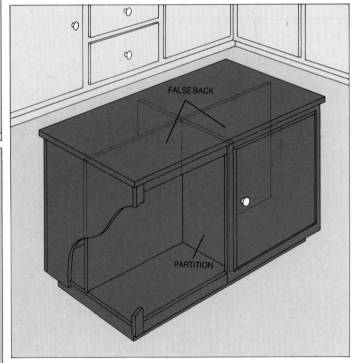

A triangular corner cabinet. The parts of this unit, traditionally used as a display cabinet, are laid out like those of the corner cabinet on pages 11–12, but fit together differently. The sides meet in a rebate joint at the rear *(inset)* and are housed for a fixed shelf. At the front, the edges of the sides have 45-degree bevels that fit flush with the top and bottom, and the edges of the face frame are bevelled to fit flush against the walls. In the popular design shown here, two types of door *(page 37)* are used: panelled doors, which provide access to storage space at the bottom, and glass doors, which protect the display shelves above.

Cutting the Parts with a Portable Saw

Two self-aligning jigs. To cut down large panels, make a jig from two 2440 mm boards. Cut one 100 mm wide so that you retain a factory-cut edge, and screw it to the second strip, 300 mm wide, with the factory-cut edge inside and the other along one edge of the wide strip *(right)*. Clamp the pieces to a workbench with the wide piece on the bottom and overhanging the edge of the bench, set the saw on the wide piece, and use the factory-cut edge of the narrow piece as a guide to cut a strip from the wide one.

Make a jig for crosscutting in the same way, but use boards 1220 mm long, that is the width of a normal panel.

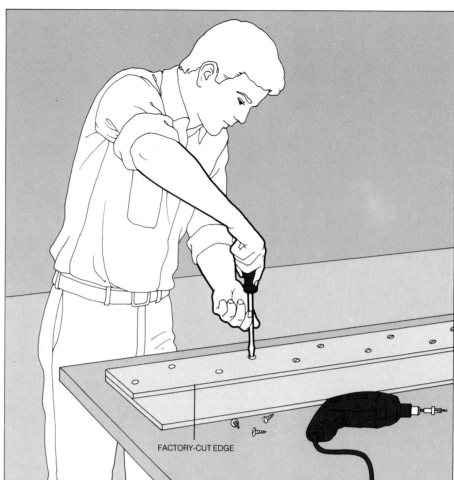

FACTORY-CUT EDGE

Making the cuts. Set two 100 by 50s about 900 mm apart on a pair of sawhorses and place the panel, good face down, on the 100 by 50s. Align the cut edge of the jig with the cutting marks at each end of the panel, clamp the jig to the panel, and set the toe of the saw against the guide with the blade 3 mm deeper than the bottom of the panel. Start the saw and push the blade slowly through the board, holding the base plate tight against the guide. Be sure that both pieces are well supported at the end of the cut, otherwise they will bind on the blade.

Working with Panels on a Table Saw

Ripping long pieces. Adjust the rip fence in the correct position for the cut and set the blade 3 mm higher than the thickness of the panel, then rest the end of the sheet on the edge of the table and ask a helper to turn the saw on. While you hold the sheet perfectly level, get your helper to push it tight against the rip fence; now slowly feed it through the blade. At the middle of the cut get your helper to move to the far side of the table to support the cut pieces as they slide off the table; the helper should not try to lift them up or pull them through the saw. Finish the cut with a push stick as for an ordinary rip cut *(page 14, centre)*, and when both pieces are beyond the blade, get the helper to pull them off the table.

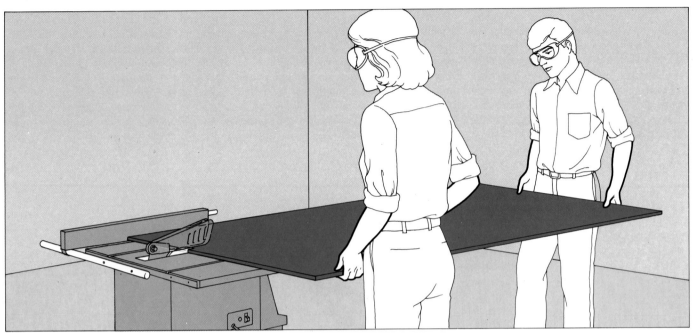

Crosscutting panels. To cut a long panel less than 450 mm wide, fasten an auxiliary fence to the metal rip fence as you would for cutting down a board *(page 14, centre)*. Adjust the rip fence for the length of the cut, set the edge of the board on the table in front of the blade and, if the board is more than 1200 mm long, get a helper to support the end of the board. Slowly feed the board through the blade, keeping it square and tight against the false fence. Make sure your helper supports the panel's weight without moving it sideways *(above)*.

Do not crosscut a long panel less than 450 mm wide without an auxiliary fence: the panel could get wedged between the blade and the rip fence. If the panel is more than 450 mm wide, treat the cut as a rip cut: the weight of the panel will prevent it getting wedged.

The Craft of Cutting Joints: Housings, Grooves and Rebates

The different pieces of the cabinets illustrated on pages 16–19 fit together in tight interlocking joints. Some of the joints are made at channels—called housings when they run across the grain and grooves when they run with the grain—while others are made at stepped edges called rebates. Both kinds of joint are generally 19 mm wide and 6 mm deep. These classic woodworking joints strengthen a cabinet by increasing the gluing area, and they make the pieces easy to assemble and align. The strength of the joints themselves depends on the precision of the tool that is used to make the cuts.

A router fitted with a 19 mm straight bit makes both housing and rebate cuts with razor-sharp precision. To make sure the cuts run in a perfectly straight line, you will need to use a straightedge guide *(opposite page, above)*. Hold the router firmly—it tends to twist away from you—start every cut with the bit clear of the wood to be cut, and move the router at a moderate speed from left to right.

Because a router is portable and can be placed anywhere on the work, it is particularly useful for cutting housings that are difficult to reach, such as those in a fixed shelf in the middle of a tall cabinet or bookcase. At other locations a table saw does the same job in less time than the router, and with about the same degree of precision. General techniques for the table saw are described on pages 13–15.

To make housing, groove and rebate cuts with a table saw, you can fit it either with a one-blade assembly called a wobbler, or with a more precise accessory called a dado headset, which consists of a set of blades of different thicknesses. The width of a dado headset cut is determined by the number of inner blades, called spacers; on most models, fine adjustments of the width are made with paper washers inserted between the spacers. A home-made attachment called a springboard, which is fitted to the rip fence of the table saw, holds the piece to be cut down and against the blade. When the saw is used to cut rebates, an additional jig—a wooden fence with a rounded notch *(page 24, Step 4)*—prevents the blade touching the metal fence.

To use a dado headset, the riving knife has to be taken out from behind the blade. On some models of table saw, the crown guard can remain in place, but on models where the crown guard holds the knife in position, the guard will have to be removed as well. Extreme caution must be used to keep hands safely away from the very sharp exposed blades.

Whichever tool you use, begin by grouping together the cabinet pieces that need matching joints, using your working drawings to determine the cuts for each piece. Mark the position and width of each cut, using one piece as a template to mark those with duplicate joints. If you are using a router, mark guidelines *(below)* in the same way. Use your template as a sample: make the cuts it requires, then recheck the position of the marked cuts on other pieces in the same group.

If you use a table saw, set the blade and rip fence for one cut and cut all pieces with the same joint before resetting the blade and fence. On each piece, cut the rebate joints first. Double-check the positions of the housings and grooves using the inside edges of the rebates as reference points, then cut the housings that run across the board. Finish by cutting the grooves that run down the board.

Making Housings, Grooves and Rebates with a Router

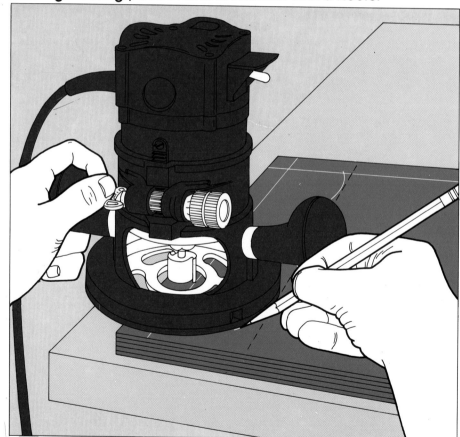

Positioning a guide. Mark the positions and widths of the channels and rebates on the board using two lines for a housing or groove, one for a rebate. Set the router bit flush with the base, and place the router near the board edge that is to be cut, with the bit centred in the marked channel or rebate. Trace the outline of the router base, trace a second outline near the opposite edge of the board and, using a straightedge, draw a guideline between the two at the points farthest from the cutting lines for the housing, groove or rebate.

Sand and wax the edge of a straight piece of plywood that is 150 mm wide and is cut to the length of the joint. Fasten the marked board to a workbench, using a G-cramp and, if necessary, a 40 mm nail driven part way in. Set the waxed edge of the guide along the guideline and clamp or nail the guide to the board.

Cutting a rebate. After fastening the board and guide in place, set the base of the router on the board, with the bit clear of the wood and 50 mm in from the left end. Turn the power on and push the bit into the wood, towards the rebate line, until the base of the router meets the edge of the guide; then move the router from left to right, pressing it firmly against the guide *(below)*. Complete the cut by moving the router from right to left through the uncut 50 mm of the rebate.

Cutting a housing or groove. Place the router with its base against the guide and its bit clear of the left edge of the wood. Turn the power on, push the bit into the wood and move the router along the guide until the bit clears the right edge.

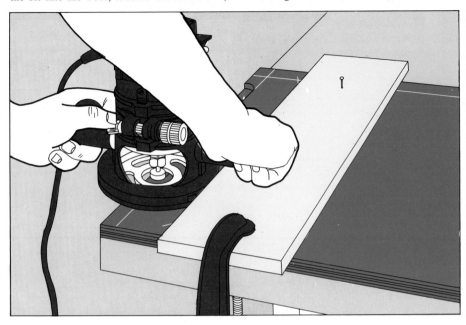
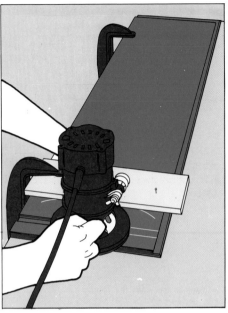

A Dado Headset on a Table Saw

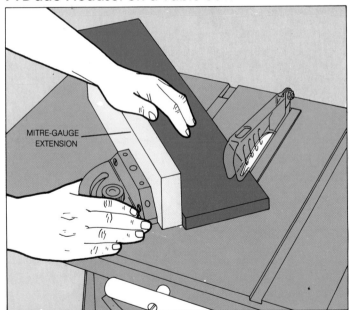

MITRE-GAUGE EXTENSION

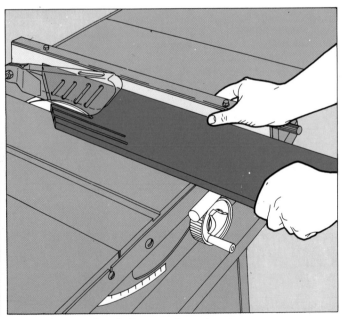

1 Mitring the springboard. Use the table saw as shown on pages 13–15 to cut a piece of solid wood 19 mm thick, 600 mm long and 125 mm wide, for the springboard; then fit the mitre gauge with a smooth wood extension, set the gauge at a 45-degree angle and hold the cut board against the extension with your left hand. Start the saw; push the gauge forwards with your right hand to cut the wood about 125 mm in from the end.

2 Slotting the springboard. Remove the mitre gauge, fasten the rip fence 120 mm from the blade and cut a slot 125 mm deep in the mitred end of the springboard. Cut identical slots at 5 mm intervals, moving the fence 5 mm closer to the blade before each cut.

3 **Attaching the dado headset.** With the table saw unplugged, remove the standard blade, table insert and riving knife; if your guard is attached to the knife, remove the guard as well. Install an outside blade of the dado headset on the arbor and add spacers and, if necessary, paper washers to bring the interior of the head to the correct width. Set the other outside blade on the arbor, replace the arbor washer and screw the arbor nut loosely in place.

Adjust the blades so that the larger teeth of one outside blade are opposite the smaller teeth of the other, and the spacers line up with gullets of both blades (inset), then tighten the arbor nut. Install a wide-slotted dado insert in the saw table.

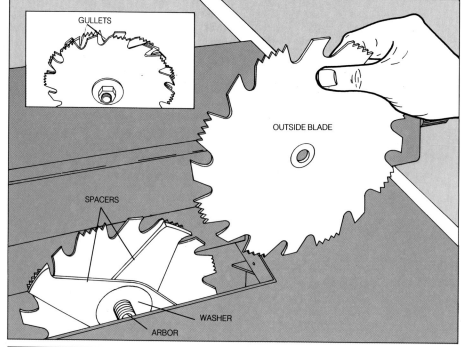

4 **Notching a fence for the rebate cuts.** Lower the dado headset to the level of the table. Fit the metal rip fence with a wooden auxiliary fence 150 mm high and 19 mm thick. Position the wooden fence so that 6 mm of its thickness overlaps the dado headset; then turn the power on and slowly raise the dado headset about 12 mm by turning the blade-height crank to cut a rounded notch in the wooden fence. Turn off the power and lower the blade.

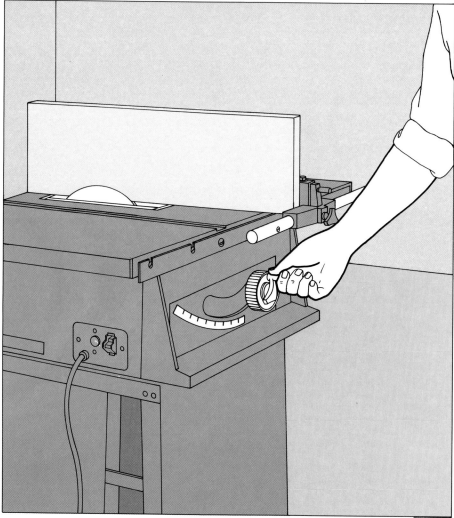

5 **Setting up the springboard.** Place a narrow timber offcut as thick as the cabinet pieces between the fence and the dado headset. Clamp the springboard to the fence with its slotted edge resting on the timber offcut and directly over the dado headset. Check the setting of the springboard by moving the offcut forwards along the fence; the springboard fingers should snap back and forth. Remove the timber offcut.

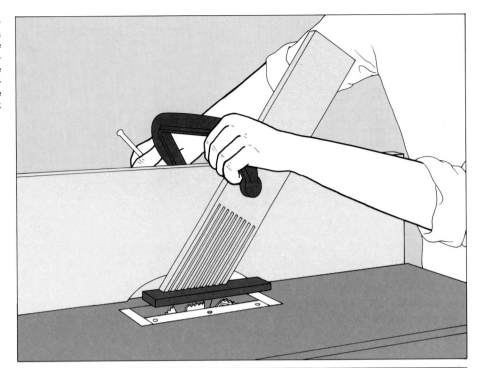

6 **Making the cuts.** To cut a rebate *(right)*, raise the dado headset, turn the power on, set the cabinet piece on the infeed side of the table with its edge against the fence, and slowly push the board forwards over the dado headset and under the springboard. Cut a housing or groove near the edge of a board in the same way, but position the fence as for a rip cut.

To cut a housing or groove in the middle of a board *(right, below)*, clamp a wooden stop block to the table or to the rip fence near the front of the saw to set the location of the housing or groove; then fit the mitre gauge with an auxiliary fence. Turn the power on, place the board on the infeed side of the table and with its edge against the stop block; push the gauge slowly forwards towards the dado headset with your right hand, while holding the board firmly down and against the gauge with your left.

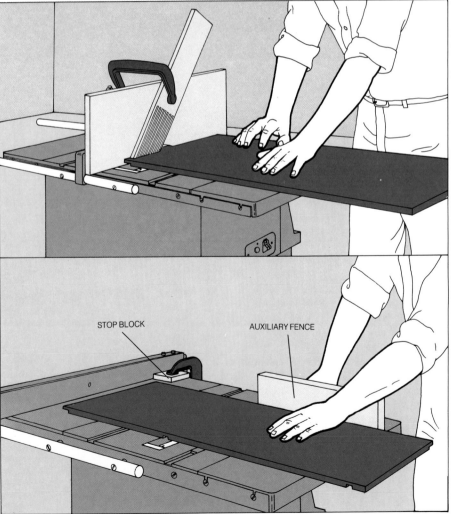

STOP BLOCK

AUXILIARY FENCE

Putting the Pieces Together

Wall-mounted and base cabinets are assembled in much the same way, though a base cabinet requires a few additional steps *(pages 28–29)*. After the housings, grooves and rebates have been cut *(pages 22–25)*, the pieces are assembled face down on the workshop floor over protective sheets of cardboard or scrap plywood, and fastened together with PVA glue and nails or screws. The entire job must be done within two or three hours, so that the pieces are aligned and the back installed before the glue sets.

A warp in a piece may keep it from fitting neatly into a housing or groove; if necessary, enlist a helper to pop the joint together, or make braces to force the bowed piece straight *(page 29, top)*.

If any joints are loose, apply enough glue to fill the gaps. To achieve perfect joints, take care at the cutting stage. For precise rebates, measure the thickness of the boards before you cut the joints so that you can adjust the width accordingly. In the case of housing joints, make the housing 0.6 mm narrower than the board it is to house. Then use a smoothing plane to chamfer a 0.5 mm shaving across each end of the board that is to be housed.

After gluing, secure the pieces together using lost-head or oval nails. When fixing into end grain, drive the nails in at opposing angles—called dovetailing—to give greater holding power.

Nails driven into plywood edges sometimes hit knots—which can deflect a nail through the finished face of the cabinet—or a hollow spot. Do not attempt to drive the nail or correct its course: pull it out and use another one about 25 mm away.

When you are working with chipboard and blockboard, use chipboard screws; the fully threaded shanks will reduce the risk of joints pulling apart. As an extra precaution, dip each screw in glue before securing it in the pilot hole.

Assembling a Wall-Mounted Cabinet

1 **Test-fitting the pieces.** Get a helper to hold a cabinet side on edge on the floor, front side down, while you slide the bottom into its housing; if necessary, hold a block of timber against the side over the housing and tap the block gently with a hammer to slide the housing securely home. Set the bottom into its housing in the other cabinet side, slide the top into the rebates in the sides, then finally slide the partition into its housings in the top and bottom. Measure the actual dimensions of the cabinet and inspect all the joints; if the dimensions are wrong, recut the parts.

Take the cabinet apart and mark lines across the top, bottom and sides, opposite the middle of each housing. Starting 25 mm from the end of each housing, drive 50 mm lost-head nails part way in along the lines every 100 mm.

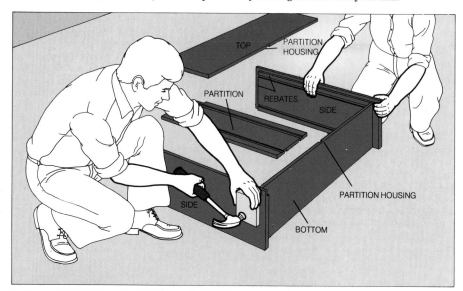

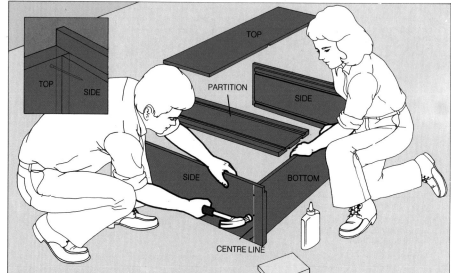

2 **Fastening the carcass.** Squeeze 3 mm beads of glue in the housing in one side and on to the end of the cabinet bottom and slide the two pieces together, front edges on the floor. Drive the nails started in Step 1 into the bottom, then glue and nail the other side to the bottom. Wipe off any excess glue immediately with a wet rag.

Apply glue beads to the rebate at the top of each side and to the ends of the top; slide these pieces tightly together and drive nails through the top into the sides *(inset)*. If the top of the cabinet is to be covered by moulding or a fascia *(pages 50–51)*, also nail through the side into the end of the top. Finally, apply glue to the ends of the partition and to its housings in the top and bottom, slide the partition down into the housings and drive the nails (started in Step 1) into the ends of the partition.

3 **Squaring the cabinet.** Working with a helper, hook the end of a steel tape measure on one corner of the cabinet and measure diagonally to the opposite corner; measure the other diagonal in the same way. If the measurements differ, push the corners used for the longer measurement towards each other and let them spring back, then re-measure both diagonals. Repeat the adjustment until the measurements are equal, then punch all the nails.

Cut a hanging rail—a piece of 18 mm board 75 mm wide—to fit snugly between the side pieces; start two 50 mm lost-head nails in each side piece opposite the ends of the hanging rail.

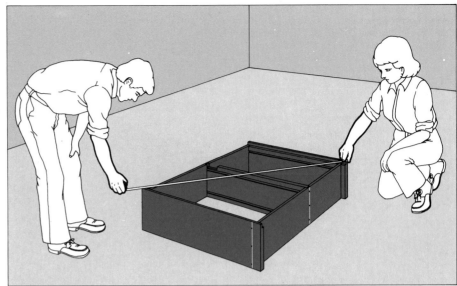

4 **Installing the hanging rail.** Apply glue beads to the top and ends of the hanging rail and to the areas it will meet at the top of the cabinet and the partition. Slide the rail into place; drive in the nails started in Step 3. Drive two nails through the rail into the partition, and nail through the cabinet top into the rail every 150 mm.

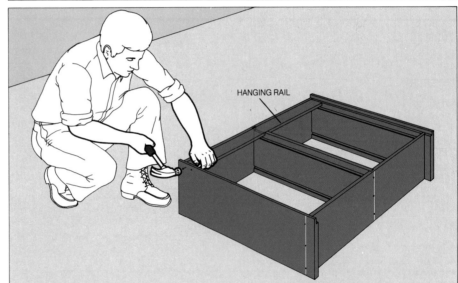

HANGING RAIL

5 **Aligning the cabinet.** Make sure the cabinet is square *(Step 3)*—adjust it if necessary. Check that the floor on which the cabinet is resting is flat, then sight from the top edge of one side piece to the edge of the other near each corner. If one corner is higher than the others *(inset)*, because of a warp in the cabinet, weigh down the raised corner until it is flat against the floor. If the floor is not flat, raise the low corner on shims and weigh down the high corners. Leave the shims and weights in place until the glue has dried.

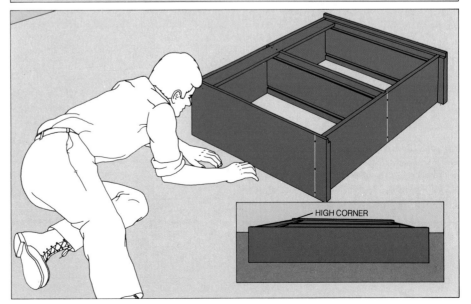

HIGH CORNER

6 Attaching the back. Glue and nail a 6 mm plywood or hardboard back cut to fit flush with the outer edges of the top and bottom and between the rebates in the sides. Apply the glue sparingly to the sides, top, bottom, partition and hanging bar, but not to the back itself; use 25 mm panel pins or round-wire nails, driven through the back at 75 mm intervals into the sides, top, bottom and partition, with the side nails angled slightly outwards. Drive two rows of nails through the back into the hanging bar.

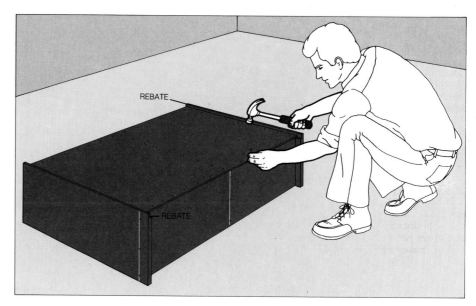

The Specialized Parts of a Base Cabinet

Making the base. Nail together a base of front and back pieces, end pieces and interior braces called bearers. For the front and back, use strips of 130 by 18 mm board—if both ends will be concealed by the walls, cut the strips to the length of the cabinet; if one end is exposed cut them 75 mm shorter; if both are exposed, cut them 150 mm shorter. For the ends and bearers, use strips 110 mm less than the cabinet width for a standard cabinet, 180 mm less for an island cabinet or room divider. Nail ends, front and back together, then nail bearers to front and back pieces, so that there will be a bearer below each partition, plus a bearer between partitions, and between partitions and sides. At each end set a horizontal screwing strip *(page 17)* of 100 by 18 mm board, flush with the bottom of the frame, and nail it to front, back and side pieces.

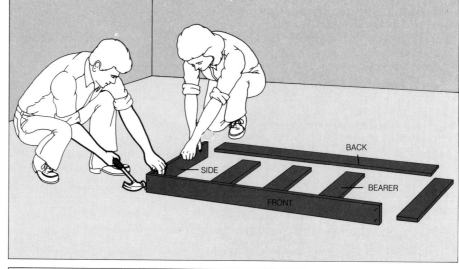

Installing drawer supports. Before installing the cabinet back *(Step 6, above)*, nail drawer-support strips of 18 mm board, 100 mm wide, between the housings in the sides and partition. Working down from the top of the cabinet, fasten a strip below each drawer opening, flush with the cabinet front, using glue and 37 mm lost-head nails at each end; then fasten another drawer-support strip flush with the back edge.

If the drawer supports fit into matching housings on both sides of a partition, fasten the strips on one side with 37 mm lost-head nails driven straight into their ends, then fasten the strips on the other side with 37 mm lost-head nails toenailed through the support strip, into the partition, and on into the support strip *(inset)*.

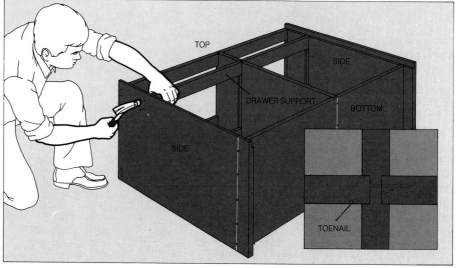

Temporary Braces for Fixed Shelves

Inserting the braces. After installing the fixed shelves for a floor-to-ceiling cabinet by the same method as used for installing drawer supports *(opposite page, bottom)*, tap a wooden brace—a 50 by 25 mm offcut will do—between the cabinet bottom and the middle of the shelf; to determine the length of the brace, measure the distance between the bottom and an end of the shelf. Measure between the cabinet top and the ends of the shelves, cut braces to these lengths and fit them between the top and the middle of each shelf. Install the cabinet back *(opposite page, Step 6)*, fastening it to the shelves with glue and with 25 mm panel pins or round-wire nails every 150 mm, then remove the braces.

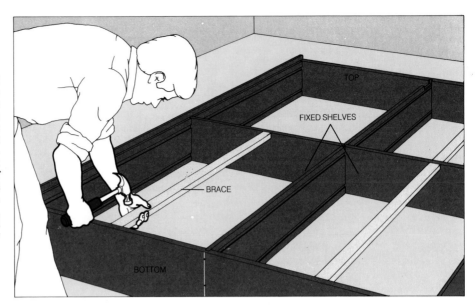

Making a Worktop

1 **Installing the supports.** After fastening the bottom to the sides *(page 26, Step 2)* glue and nail two strips of 100 by 18 mm board between the rebates at the tops of the sides. Prepare these strips by cutting matching housings for the partition across the middle of each strip; set a strip flush with the front edge, and glue and nail it to the sides *(page 26, Step 2, inset)*. Install the other strip flush with the back of the cabinet *(right)* and install the partition. Then attach the back *(opposite page, Step 6)*.

For a wooden worktop, cut a board 6 mm longer and wider than the finished cabinet and face frame. For a worktop that is to be covered with plastic laminate, cut a piece 25 mm wider than the cabinet and 25 mm longer at each exposed side, and glue and nail 19 mm butt-joined battens 25 mm wide to the bottom of the board, flush with each edge *(inset)*; nail the battens to the board in a zigzag pattern.

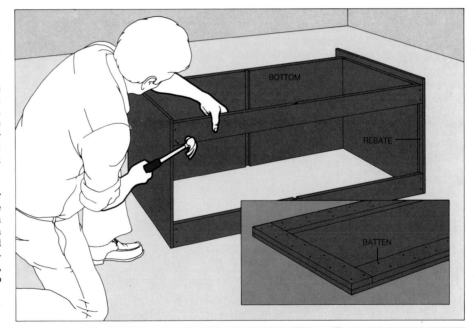

2 **Completing a wooden worktop.** Set a length of wooden lipping, 19 mm thick, 25 mm wide and mitre cut at one end, against the longest exposed edge of the top, with the mitre at an exposed corner, and mark the location of the other corner on the lipping. Make a mitre cut at the mark if the side is exposed, a square cut if it adjoins a wall. Fasten the lipping to the edge with glue and 32 mm panel pins or nails driven through pilot holes every 150 mm. Mark, cut and fasten lipping to the other exposed sides; the back edge and any side edge that adjoins a wall do not need lipping because the board will be scribed to fit the wall *(page 48, bottom)*. Do not attach the worktop until the cabinet has been secured to the base and to the wall *(pages 52–53)*.

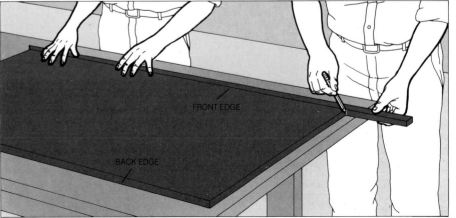

The Final Step: a Face Frame

Two Ways to Build a Frame

To provide a strong fixing base for doors and to cover any unfinished edges, the front of a well-built cabinet has a face frame of planed-all-round (PAR) solid timber, 19 mm thick and 50 mm wide (nominal). Once the pieces are cut to length, fasten them with glue and loose tongues or dowels. For a paint finish, where nail heads will be concealed, use a softwood frame secured to the carcass with glue and panel pins. For a wood finish, where appearance is important, use either softwood, or a hardwood such as ramin or sapele (African mahogany) and glue the frame to the carcass.

Cut with special precision for tiny errors multiply as more cuts are made. Follow a pencil sketch based on the measurements of each piece of the cabinet carcass—the top and sides of the cabinet without its face frame. To saw the pieces, use a stop block *(page 14, top, inset)* rather than a guideline. To calculate the lengths of the frame pieces, follow these rules:

☐ The top of the top rail should be flush with the carcass top.

☐ The top of the bottom rail should be flush with the carcass floor.

☐ Side stiles are generally 28 mm longer than the height of the carcass.

☐ The outside of an exposed stile should be flush with the carcass side.

☐ A stile that meets a wall should overhang the carcass side by at least 12 mm, to provide a scribing strip *(page 48)*; if a bank of drawers will be installed next to this stile, align the inside edge of the stile flush with the inside edge of the carcass.

☐ In a cabinet with drawers, the partition is usually offset 16 mm; the centre stile is set flush with one side of the partition.

☐ Intermediate rails are set flush with the top of the drawer supports.

☐ The simplest way to fasten the face frame together is with loose tongues—thin pieces of wood that fit into hidden slots in the ends and edges of the boards. This method leaves a slight margin for error and permits some adjustments after the joints are cut. The slots are made with a router and a special slotting bit, which cuts a groove 19 or 12 mm deep and 3 mm wide. Loose tongues can be obtained from a timber merchant or cut with a table saw. If you use the saw, rip 19 mm boards into strips that fit snugly when gently tapped into the slots, hold several strips together

and crosscut them into pieces twice the depth of the slots, less 2 mm.

Even stronger than loose tongues are dowels—birch pegs glued into holes in the joining pieces. Dowels pre-grooved with spiral glue channels are available from timber merchants and D.I.Y. shops. Dowel construction does not permit adjustments after the frame is assembled. The holes for the dowels must be marked perfectly and drilled precisely, with the help of an accurate dowelling jig.

An easy-to-cut frame. In this frame only two lengths of wood are used; all stiles are one length, all rails another. The pieces are joined by thin wooden strips called loose tongues that are glued into slots in the mating pieces. Where one side of a joint will be hidden from view—as by a worktop—the mating slots run out of the end of the stile and out of the hidden side of the rail and are connected by two loose tongues *(top inset)*. If both sides of a joint are visible—as at the end of an intermediate rail—a "blind" joint is made with slots shorter than the rail width, connected by a single loose tongue *(bottom inset)*. Dowels *(bottom of page)* can also be used to join this frame.

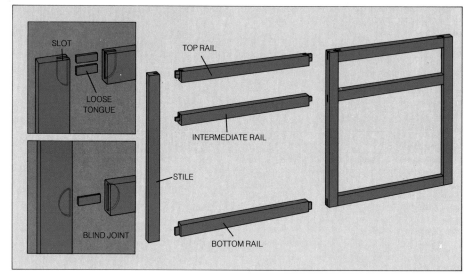

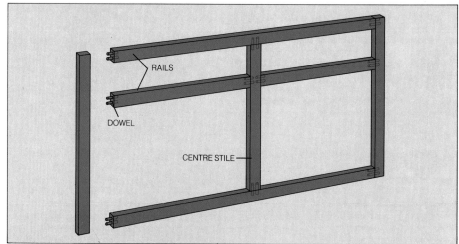

A frame with minimum joints. This design, which requires two fewer joints than the frame in the drawing above it, is generally preferred for a cabinet that is to be stained—staining leaves the joints visible, and the fewer the joints, the easier it is to achieve an attractive finish. The top and bottom rails run between the side stiles and a short centre stile fits between the rails. At each joint of this frame, two 6 mm dowels, 50 mm long, are glued into precisely aligned holes in the end of one piece and the edge of the other, fastening the two pieces together.

Making a Frame with Loose-Tongue Joints

1 **Marking the pieces.** After cutting the stiles and top and bottom rails, assemble them face up on the workbench; make a pencil mark on the face of each board and matching letters on the sides of each joint. Draw lines on the edge of each stile to mark the inside corners made by stile and rails.

If your cabinet will have intermediate rails to conceal drawer supports or fixed shelves, measure from the top of the carcass to the top of each support, mark the measured distance down from the top of a stile and mark the stile for the top and bottom of each intermediate rail. Set the other stiles beside the marked one and transfer the marks to them with a combination square *(inset)*, then reassemble the frame with the intermediate rails and mark the stile edges at the corners made by these rails.

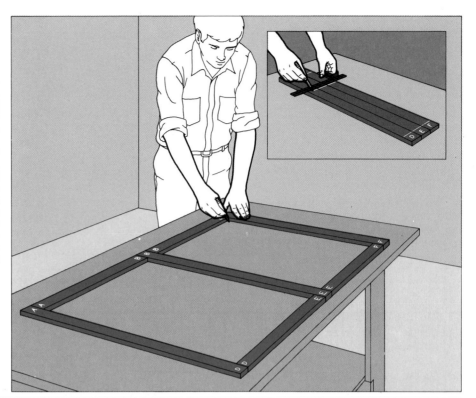

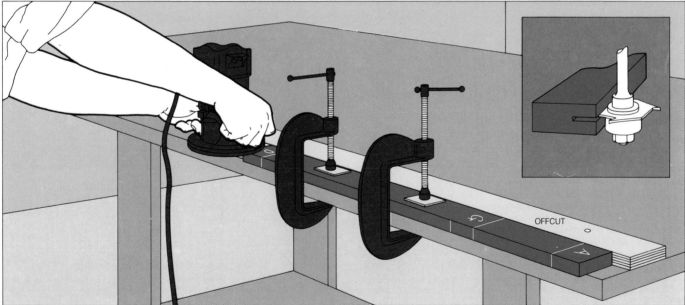

2 **Slotting the stiles.** Cut a slot in the stiles for each rail-to-stile joint, using a router fitted with a grooving cutter that makes a groove 3 mm wide and 19 or 12 mm deep.

To hold the stiles down, nail an offcut 35 mm from the edge of a workbench; clamp a stile face up beside this offcut; the stile will overhang the workbench edge. Adjust the router depth to cut the slot in the middle of the stile thickness, then turn the router on and, beginning at the left end of the stile, move the router slowly from left to right to make a shallow cut; stop the cut about

3 mm short of the mark for the edge of the rail. Make two or three more passes until the guide of the bit rolls on the edge of the stile *(inset)*.

At the right end of the board, start the slot by easing the bit into the middle of the stile thickness just within the line you have marked for the edge of the rail, then make several shallow passes with the router as you did at the other end of the board. Slot the other stiles in the same way, always moving the router from left to right. To make a blind slot for a loose tongue joint in an intermediate rail, cut a slot that does not extend

beyond the marks that indicate the edges of the intermediate rail.

To slot the rails, clamp each rail, face up, against the offcut with the end to be cut overhanging the table. Move the router very slowly from left to right, in several shallow passes—the end grain of rails is difficult to cut and can overheat the bit. If the left edge of the rail will be exposed, ease the bit into the end of the board about 3 mm from the edge and cut to the right corner; if the right edge will be exposed, start at the left corner and stop the cut just short of the edge.

3 **Inserting loose tongues into rails.** Squeeze a bead of glue into the slots of each rail, then cover the loose tongues with a thin coat of glue and tap them into the rail with a hammer. If the slot runs through one edge of the rail, as it does, for instance, at a corner hidden by a worktop, set one loose tongue flush with the edge and another inside it; for a blind slot, set one loose tongue in the slot. Let the glue set for about 30 minutes.

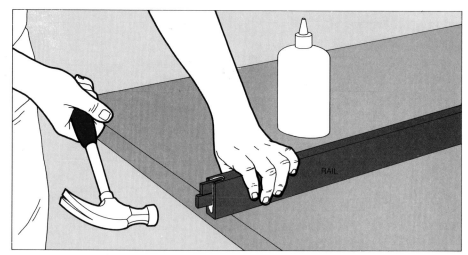

4 **Fixing rails to stiles.** Fasten each rail to one of the side stiles by first applying glue to one of the end slots of the stile and additional glue to the loose tongues at the end of the matching rail. Then set the stile on edge and work the loose tongues part way into the stile by rocking the rail from side to side. Set a block of wood on the other end of the rail and tap the rail home with a hammer.

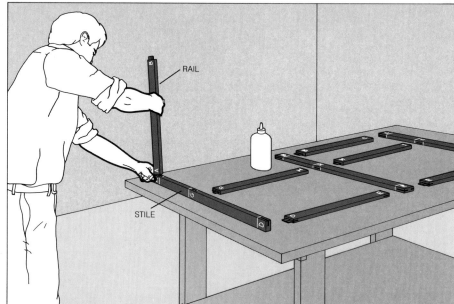

5 **Completing the joints.** After applying a coat of glue to the loose tongues at the free ends of the rails and a bead of glue to the slots in the centre stile, fit the stile on to the loose tongues. Get a helper to hold the rails steady while you rock the stile part way on to the loose tongues; then, working from one end, tap the stile on to the rails with a hammer and a block of wood. Set the completed section of the face frame on the floor, install the remaining rails in the centre stile, then install the remaining side stile as you did the centre one.

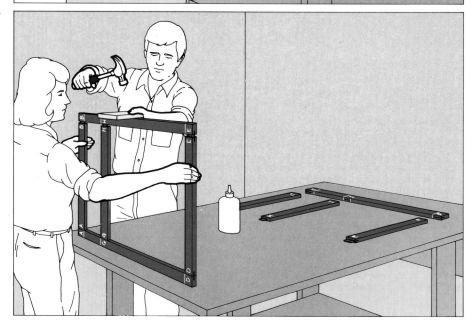

6 **Clamping the frame.** Set the frame across a workbench, overhanging each side, and fasten sash cramps round the outer stiles, directly over the top and bottom rails; protect the stiles with scraps of wood. Tighten the cramps until glue is forced out of the joints, then measure the diagonals of the frame *(page 27, Step 3)* to make sure it is square; if it is not, reset the cramps at a slight angle to the rails to pull the frame into square. When the frame is square, sight across the top for twists; if necessary, pull the lower corner sharply to bring it into line. When the frame is square and properly aligned, reverse about a quarter of a turn on each cramp.

If your frame has intermediate rails, turn the clamped frame over, rest the cramps on the workbench and fasten an additional cramp across each intermediate rail.

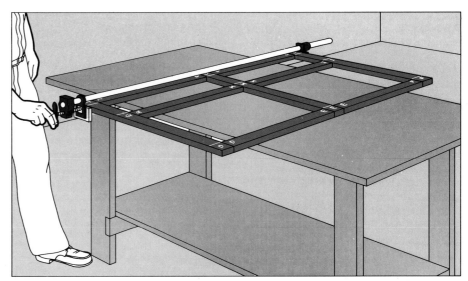

7 **Securing the frame in place.** Set the carcass of the cabinet flat on its back, set the frame in place and check the fit, particularly at exposed edges *(right)*. If the frame projects beyond edges that should be flush, plane the wood to fit after installation. If the frame is too small, line it up at the edge that gets the most exposure.

If you are going to paint the cabinet, glue the frame to the edges of the carcass. Then drive in 37 mm panel pins every 150 mm, starting at a corner where the frame and carcass must line up—for example, the bottom corner at an exposed end. Check the alignment of the frame and carcass before you drive in each pin. Work along each side and do not drive in pins at the far corner until the side is completed. After the outer sides, pin the centre stile and intermediate rails.

For a wood finish, glue the frame to the carcass and hold it securely in position with sash cramps until the glue has dried.

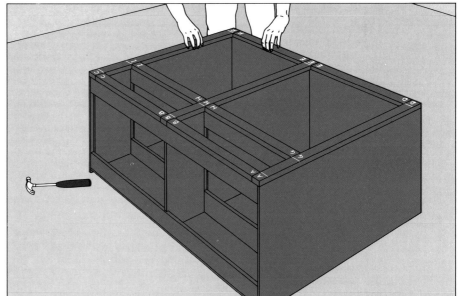

Drilling for Dowelled Joints

Marking the holes. After marking the joints *(page 31, Step 1)*, set the side stiles side by side, with the joint marks upwards; clamp the stiles together and mark their edges for the hole centres. Draw lines across all of the edges simultaneously with a combination square, 10 and 35 mm from each end *(right)*; mark for intermediate rails 12 mm from each rail edge. Clamp the rails together in the same way, and mark across the ends, 12 mm from each edge; if a stile runs into the centre of a rail, mark the joint as you marked the stiles with intermediate rails.

Centre a dowelling jig on each mark *(inset)* and drill a 6 mm hole 30 mm deep. Glue dowels into the holes and assemble rails and stiles as for loose tongues *(opposite page and above)*.

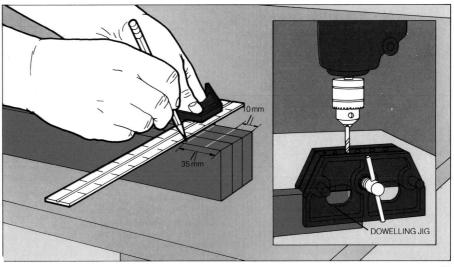

DOWELLING JIG

Fitting a Cabinet with Drawers and Doors

Doors and drawers transform shelves into a finished cabinet. A door *(pages 37–41)* encloses the cabinet; a set of drawers organizes its space and makes its contents accessible. As the only moving parts of a typical cabinet, drawers and doors are subject to great stress and must be constructed with strong joints and materials.

The materials that are most commonly used for making drawer backs, sides and fronts are timber, plywood or veneered chipboard, at least 12 mm thick for backs and sides, and 16 mm thick for fronts. These pieces can be put together in a variety of different ways, using any type of connection from the simple butt joint to the sophisticated dovetail joint. The majority of built-in drawers use a compromise between these two extremes—a standardized pattern of rebates and housings that can be cut with a router, a table saw *(opposite)* or even a handsaw and chisel.

The technique of drawer construction is also influenced by the style of the drawer front. The simplest to make and most commonly employed is the lipped drawer front, which has a rebated edge that overlaps the cabinet frame. Because the overlap conceals any irregularities of fit between the drawer and its opening, this type of drawer requires no finicky sanding and planing.

Less common, because of the difficulty of achieving the exact fit required, is the flush drawer, whose front fits inside the cabinet so that the cabinet surface remains smooth, uninterrupted by projections. For this style you must cut the front precisely to the size of the drawer opening and then painstakingly trim it with a block plane and sandpaper to create equal clearances of 1 mm all round the drawer. If you install both doors and drawers in a single cabinet or a set of cabinets, use the same style, overlapping or flush, for both.

Drawers stronger than those ordinarily constructed can be made by using different joints. For example, cutting grooves in the sides to hold a rebated front, forming a bare-faced housing joint, will create a stronger joint and adds rigidity, but requires that you glue and screw a false front to the drawer to cover the end grain of the sides. Another strong joint is the interlocking tongued joint *(right, inset)*. Trickier to make than the bare-faced housing joint, this joint creates a larger gluing area and,

because the side end grain is covered, does not require a false front, thus making it suitable for flush doors.

The mechanism that guides a drawer's movement is critical to the overall dimensions of the drawer. Traditionally the drawers in fine furniture slide on wooden runners, but in modern built-in cabinets commercial metal glides are very often preferred for their sturdiness and ease of installation. Glides require extra space—specified by the manufacturer but generally 12 mm—between the drawer sides and the opening edges, and the drawer front must extend beyond the sides in order to conceal the hardware.

In the course of construction, test-fit drawer pieces and check them for squareness before you glue, clamp and nail the joints together.

Basic Drawer Designs

The lipped drawer. Fit the bottom into side and front grooves cut 6 mm deep and located 12 mm above the lower edges of the frame. The back rests on the bottom and fits into vertical side housings 6 mm deep, set 12 mm in from the back edges. The drawer front—cut 12 mm larger on each side than the opening—is rebated on all edges. Rebates holding the drawer sides have a depth equal to half the thickness of the front, and a width calculated by adding 9 mm (for overlap) to the thickness of a side piece plus the thickness of the glide hardware. Rebates along the top and bottom of the front are the same depth as the end rebates, and 9 mm wide. Joints are held by glue and by 32 mm lost-head nails driven at an angle through the sides and back edge of the bottom.

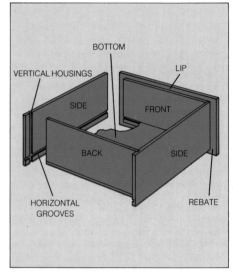

An extra-strength drawer. The two-layer front shown here adds rigidity; a construction front rebated down both edges fits into 8 mm housings cut in the sides, forming two bare-faced housing joints. A false front is then glued and screwed over the construction front. The drawer back, as well as the front and sides, is grooved to receive the drawer bottom. For flush drawers, use an interlocking tongued joint *(inset and opposite)* to join the sides and front.

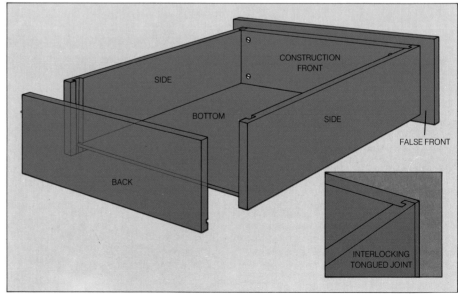

An Interlocking Tongued Joint for Extra Strength

1 **Cutting the side housings.** If you are using a table saw, mount a 6 mm dado headset *(page 24)* and clamp a stop block on a mitre gauge extension; when you butt a drawer side against the block, the left edge of the dado headset should be 12 mm from the end of the drawer side. Set the dado headset height at 6 mm, hold the drawer side with its inside face down, and cut the housing. Similarly cut the opposite drawer side.

If you use a router *(pages 22–23)* to cut the housings, fit it with a 6 mm bit, set the bit 6 mm deep and use a jig to guide the bit 12 mm from the front end of the side.

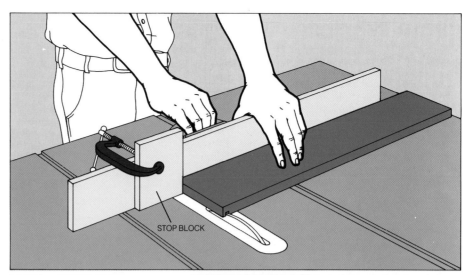

STOP BLOCK

2 **Cutting a channel in the front.** Mount a tenoning jig in the right-hand mitre slot of a table saw and clamp the drawer front in it, between wood blocks, with its inside face towards the jig and its front edge on the table. Set the height of the dado headset to 16 mm, adjust the jig so that the left edge of the dado headset is 6 mm from the inside face of the front, and push the jig along the mitre slot to cut the channel. Reposition the drawer front to cut the channel in the opposite end.

If you do not have a tenoning jig, make a substitute of three pieces of 19 mm stock, screwed together to form an inverted trough that slides on the rip fence *(inset)*, and fasten the drawer front to this home-made jig with a G-cramp. With a router, use a grooving cutter that cuts a channel 6 mm wide and 16 mm deep, and follow the techniques on page 31, Step 2.

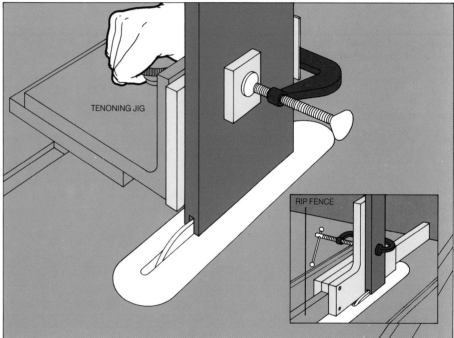

TENONING JIG

RIP FENCE

3 **Trimming the front tongues.** Set the dado headset to a height of 8 mm and butt the drawer front—with its inside face down—against a mitre-gauge extension and a stop block positioned so that the blades will cut 10 mm off the end of the board. To make the cut, hold the drawer front firmly with your left hand and push the mitre gauge with your right. Reposition the board to trim the other end, then fit the drawer front and sides together to check the joints.

If you are using a router, set the depth at 8 mm and guide the tool with a clamped board.

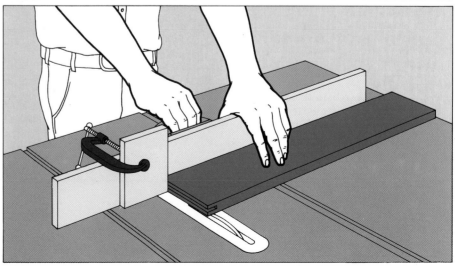

Installing Drawer Glides

1 Positioning the outer channels. For each side of a drawer opening that is not flush with the edge of the face frame, cut a spacer as long as the cabinet is deep, at least 75 mm wide, and as thick as the distance inside the cabinet from the cabinet side to the edge of the face frame. Set each spacer, edge up, on a drawer support and against the cabinet side or partition, drill pilot holes for 32 mm No. 8 screws through the spacer and into the side or partition, and screw in the spacer.

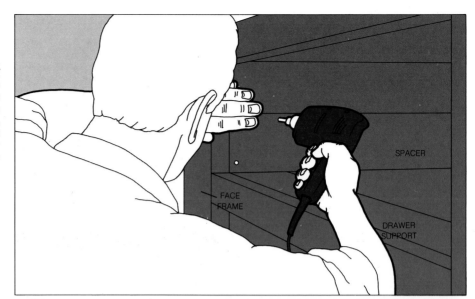

2 Mounting the glides. Set the lower edge of each outer channel flush with the lower edge of the spacer, set the front edge of the channel flush with the front of the cabinet, and mark the locations of the channel's oblong screwholes. Drill pilot holes at the marks and fasten the channel to the spacer or cabinet with the screws provided by the manufacturer.

Screw the inner channels to the sides of the drawer *(inset)* at the positions that are called for in the manufacturer's instructions.

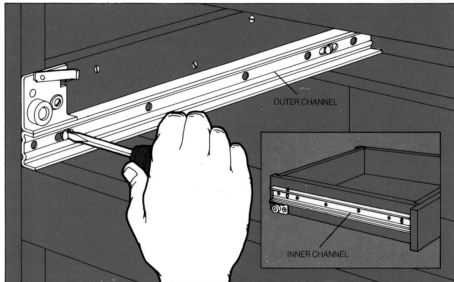

3 Adjusting the glides. Align the inner-channel tracks with the front wheels of the outer channels and slide the drawer into the cabinet opening; if the drawer is blocked by stops in the channel, tilt its front up, then slide it the rest of the way. Check the drawer's position: it should close flush against the cabinet, with straight and equal clearances round the drawer front. If it does not, loosen the inner-channel screws and move the tracks up or down to adjust the clearances, or loosen the outer-channel screws and slide the tracks forwards or back to adjust the depth of run. When the drawer fits, drill pilot holes and drive screws through the circular screwholes in the inner and outer channels.

Putting In the Doors

Choose a door that suits the use and location of the cabinet. In tight quarters, sliding doors may be preferable, because they do not open out into the space in front of a cabinet, but they have the drawback of providing access to only half the cabinet at a time. Hinged doors are more versatile and far more common. Usually installed so that they will swing on one side, they can also pivot at the top or bottom, and a door that is hinged along the bottom can double as a work surface if it is also braced by hardware such as continuous piano hinges and stay supports *(page 41)*.

On a hinged door, as on a drawer front, a lipped or overlapping fit against the cabinet front is more suitable for built-ins than a flush fit within an opening, because overlapping doors conceal any slight errors that may be made in fitting.

Ready-made cabinet doors are available at timber merchants in a variety of standard styles, but you can easily build your own. The design you choose should reflect both the quality of the cabinet and the tools at your disposal. Thus, you can simply cut a plain, flat door, or you may prefer to assemble a relatively sophisticated frame-and-panel design.

A frame-and-panel door calls for careful planning before construction: you must, for instance, add 50 mm to the length of horizontal frame pieces to allow for tenons in mortise-and-tenon joints, and subtract 6 mm from the panel to give an easy fit. When you fit the pieces of this door together, glue only the corners of the frame and allow the panel itself to "float" in the frame. A table saw simplifies and speeds the construction of a frame-and-panel door, but you can also undertake the job using only a router.

Whatever door design you choose, use the drawings and captions on pages 40–41 as a guide to the appropriate hardware. On a door with a hinged edge longer than 600 mm, install three hinges to provide additional support.

The Classic Designs for Cabinet Doors

A plain panel door. For a simple cabinet front, cut a door at least 19 mm thick. To make a lipped design, as in this illustration, cut the door 12 mm larger than the dimensions of the opening, and cut rebates on the back edges of the door to the size—generally 9 by 9 mm—of the offset of the hinges *(page 40)*. Then use a router with a rounding-over bit to round the door's exterior edges, or alternatively bevel the edges back at a 30-degree angle *(inset)*.

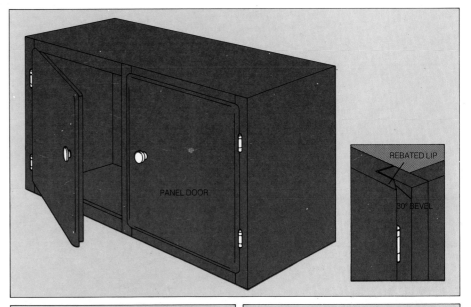

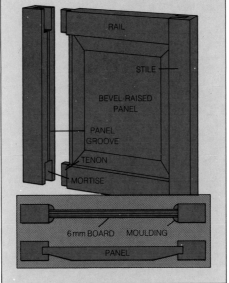

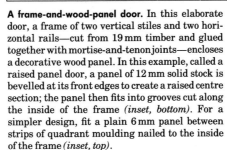

A frame-and-wood-panel door. In this elaborate door, a frame of two vertical stiles and two horizontal rails—cut from 19 mm timber and glued together with mortise-and-tenon joints—encloses a decorative wood panel. In this example, called a raised panel door, a panel of 12 mm solid stock is bevelled at its front edges to create a raised centre section; the panel then fits into grooves cut along the inside of the frame *(inset, bottom)*. For a simpler design, fit a plain 6 mm panel between strips of quadrant moulding nailed to the inside of the frame *(inset, top)*.

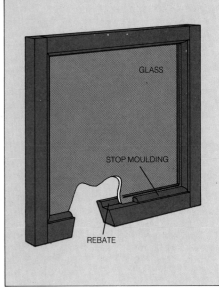

A frame-and-glass door. For a door with a panel of glass or of metal mesh, cut mortise-and-tenon joints *(pages 38–39)*, assemble and glue the frame, and then cut rebates 12 mm deep and 9 mm wide round its back edges using a router. Secure the material in the rebates with lengths of moulding nailed to the outer edges of the rebates; the width of the moulding is determined by the thickness of the panel.

Making the Frame for a Panelled Door

1 Grooving the frame pieces. To cut grooves using a table saw *(below, left)*, fit it with a 6 mm dado headset *(page 24)* and set the rip fence 12 mm from the outer blade. Raise the dado headset to a height of 12 mm, set a frame piece of 19 mm solid timber firmly in place, its inside edge down and its outside face against the rip fence. Clamp a springboard to the worktable against the frame piece so that one end is level with the front of the blade. Use a push stick to feed the piece of timber across the blades *(page 14, centre)*. In the same way, groove the other frame pieces, always with the outside face against the rip fence.

To cut these grooves with a router *(below, right)*, clamp a frame piece, inside edge up, between wood offcuts and nail stop blocks to the worktable at the sides and the right end of the assembly to steady the work. Fit the router with a 6 mm bit set to a cutting depth of 6 mm and use a router jig to guide the bit 6 mm in from the edge of the frame piece, then cut the groove.

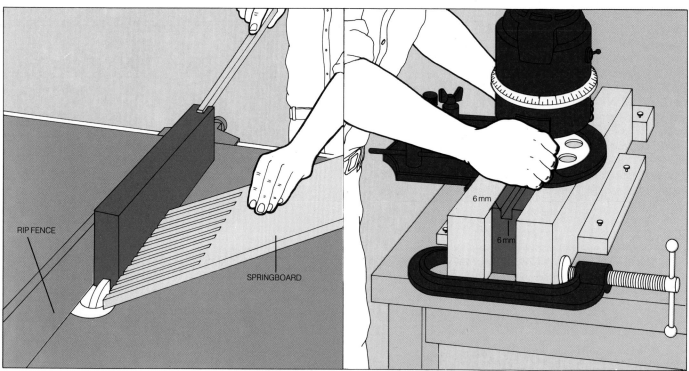

RIP FENCE

SPRINGBOARD

6 mm

6 mm

2 Mortising the stiles. Before cutting stile mortises, attach a wooden auxiliary fence to the rip fence *(page 24, Step 4)*, and set the stile in front of the blade. Then, to prevent the stile pushing up, nail a 15 by 15 mm stop block to the wooden fence; it should rest lightly on the stile and hang over the blade. Clamp the springboard to the table against the stile. Reset the dado headset to 28 mm and move the stile a short distance against the blades. Then remove the stile to measure the straight section of the mortise (the dado headset cuts a mortise round at one end; do not include the rounded end when measuring the mortise). When the straight section equals the width of the rail less 6 mm, mark the stop block at the end of the stile as a stopping point when you feed the wood for the remaining mortises.

To cut the mortises with a router, follow the techniques for grooving but make repeated passes, increasing the cutting depth of the bit by maximum increments of 9 mm, until you have deepened the cuts to 28 mm at the stile ends.

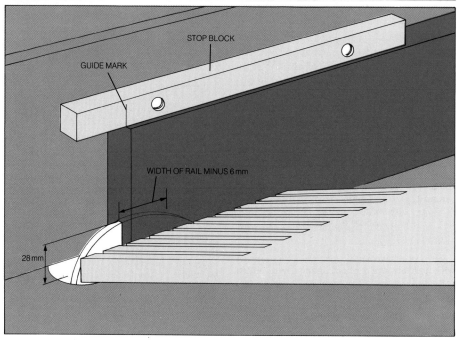

STOP BLOCK

GUIDE MARK

WIDTH OF RAIL MINUS 6 mm

28 mm

3 **Cutting tenons on the rails.** If you are using a table saw *(below)*, fit it with an ordinary blade set to a cutting depth of 6 mm. Use the mitre gauge *(page 14)* to cut across both faces of a rail along marked lines—called shoulder lines—25 mm in from each end. To complete the tenons *(below, right)*, secure the rail vertically in a commercial or home-made tenoning jig *(page 35, Step 2)*, ad-

just the jig for a cut 6 mm in from the outer face of the rail, set the blade height to 25 mm and run the rail across the blade to make a "cheek" cut. Turn the rail round to cut a second cheek, completing the tenon.

To make tenons with a router, cut rebates 6 mm deep and 25 mm wide, using the techniques described on pages 22–23.

When all the frame pieces are shaped, test-assemble them and sand or chisel them as necessary to achieve a perfect fit. Cut a panel 6 mm smaller on each side than the distance between the bottoms of the grooves on opposite sides, bevelling the panel if desired as explained below. Assemble the panel and frame, gluing only the mortise and tenon joints.

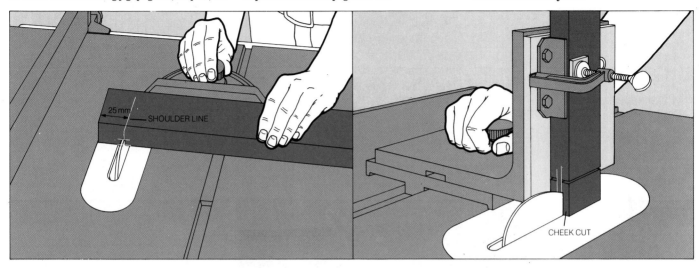

25 mm ← SHOULDER LINE

CHEEK CUT

Bevelling the Panel

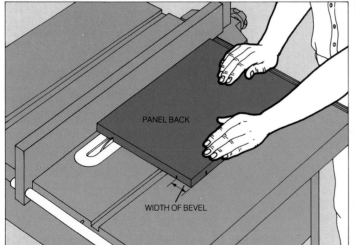

PANEL BACK

WIDTH OF BEVEL

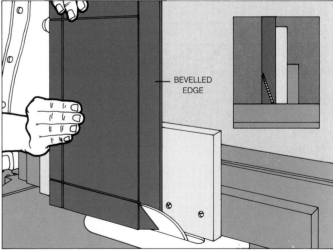

BEVELLED EDGE

1 **Starting the bevel.** When using a table saw remove the blade guard and the riving knife, set the blade to a cutting depth of 2 mm and position the rip fence so that the distance between it and the blade equals the width of the panel bevel—generally about 50 mm. Hold the panel face down, with one edge flush against the rip fence, and cut along its face; repeat these cuts on the other three edges.

If you do not have a table saw, use a circular saw with its blade at a depth of 2 mm; clamp a guide to the panel to make a straight cut.

2 **Cutting the bevel.** Move the rip fence of the table saw to the left of the blade and secure a tall auxiliary fence to it *(page 24, Step 4)*. Holding the panel with its back against the fence and its edge along the blade, adjust the fence position, blade projection and blade tilt for a cut like that in the inset. The blade should enter the edge 5 mm from the panel back and emerge from the front just below the cut made in Step 1. Keeping both hands well above the blade, slide the panel along the fence to cut the bevels round all four edges, then sand them smooth.

If you use a router, fit it with a bevelling bit and cut sharp, 30-degree bevels on the panel edges.

Hardware for Hinged Doors

A butt hinge. For flush doors that have frames of solid timber, the most commonly used hinge resembles those used on house doors, and consists of two rectangular leaves that pivot on a central pin. The leaves of a butt hinge are recessed, or mortised, into the face frame of the cabinet. Use loose-pin butt hinges, which permit you to pull out the pin and remove the door without having to unscrew the leaves.

A flush hinge. When the cabinet door is closed, this hinge folds into one thin plane eliminating the need to recess the leaves. The flush hinge is easy to install and may be used for fitting both flush and overlapping doors that do not have to carry a heavy weight.

An offset hinge. For cabinets made entirely of manufactured board—which does not securely hold screws set into its edges, required when fitting butt hinges—offset or shutter hinges permit fastening to the board surfaces, as in this overlapping door. All offset hinges have to be mortised rather than surface-mounted; the offset leaf is available in various sizes to match standard board thicknesses.

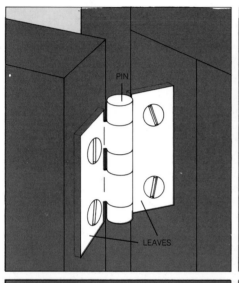

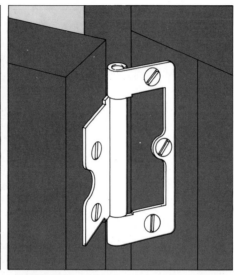

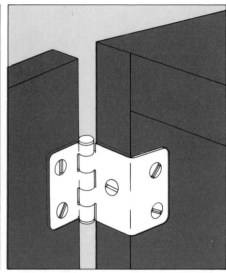

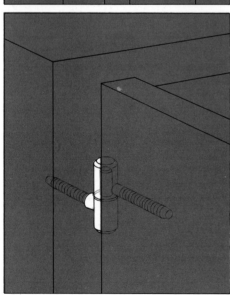

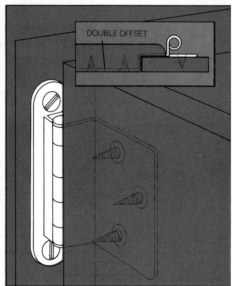

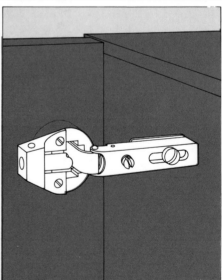

A screw-in pivot hinge. Widely used for both rebated and overlapping doors, the pivot hinge is strong and easy to fit. Its long arms make it suitable for both timber and manufactured board. The arms are screwed into holes drilled into the edge of the door and frame: the pinned arm must always be fitted to the frame. The door can be removed easily by lifting the top butt off the pin.

A semi-concealed hinge. Designed for lipped (rebated) and for partially overlapping doors, this hinge has one leaf surface-mounted on the face of the cabinet and an offset leaf mortised into the back of the door. For the overlapping door in this example, the door leaf has an offset like that of a shutter hinge; on a lipped door *(inset)* the hinge has a double offset. Buy the hinges for a lipped door before rebating the door, then you will be able to rebate the lip to a depth that exactly matches the offset of the hinge.

A concealed spring hinge. More expensive than other hinges and trickier to install, concealed spring hinges are fitted to doors in a way that makes them completely invisible when the door is shut *(page 110)*. They need no clearance since they project the door outwards without disturbing the neighbouring doors, allowing them to be used for adjacent cabinets with overlapping doors that open alongside each other. A door fitted with these hinges does not need a catch as the integral spring holds the door shut.

40

Hardware for extra support. On a very heavy door, and on a door that is subjected to special strain when opened, use a continuous or piano hinge—essentially a surface-mounted butt hinge that runs the entire length of the door. In this example a door drops down to become a work surface; the open, cantilevered door would bounce without the folding stay supports, which are screwed to the side of the cabinet and the back of the door to provide reinforcement and stability. Stay supports can also be used to control the swing of a conventional door.

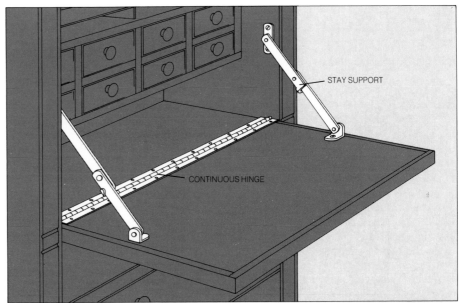

STAY SUPPORT

CONTINUOUS HINGE

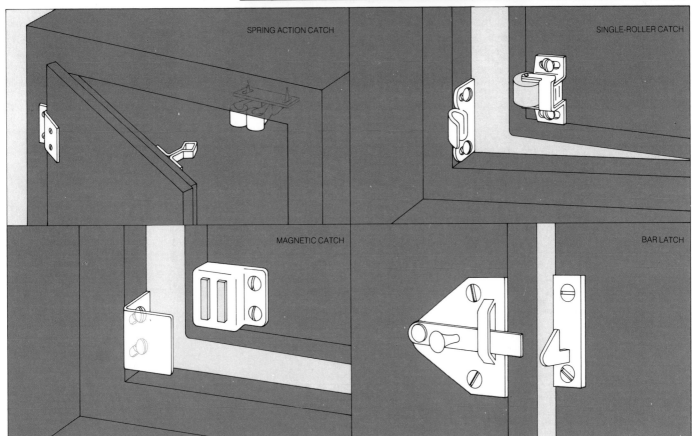

SPRING ACTION CATCH

SINGLE-ROLLER CATCH

MAGNETIC CATCH

BAR LATCH

Catches and latches. Each of these pieces of hardware has a characteristic method of installation and special advantages and disadvantages. A spring-action catch *(top left)* calls for the alignment of an arrow-shaped strike, mounted on the door, with spring-loaded double rollers mounted inside the cabinet; the assembly is durable and relatively quiet. On a single-roller catch *(top right)*, the roller is on the door and fits into a keep plate mounted on the cabinet; this catch is very quiet because it holds the closed door slightly away from the cabinet. In a magnetic catch *(bottom left)* the parts do not need to align exactly, but the catch is noisy and the magnet gradually weakens with age. An alternative to all of these concealed catches is exterior hardware, such as a bar latch *(bottom right)*; this latch serves as a door pull as well as a catch.

Tough, Long-Lasting Finishes for Built-Ins

Built-ins can be finished like conventional furniture, with oils, lacquer, shellac or wax, but they generally get harder use and require more durable finishing.

In the kitchen, a finish must resist stains from spilled food and worktops must take the scorching heat of ovenware just off the stove; in bathrooms, the finish is exposed to steam and constant moisture, and throughout the house built-in surfaces must resist abrasion, chipping and scratching. Coatings and worktops particularly suited to such heavy-duty use are described in the charts below and opposite.

Because most built-ins combine manufactured board with solid timber, special care is necessary in matching the finishes. Punch nails well below the surface and, if using a paint finish, apply a coat of aluminium primer. Fill nicks and nail holes with wood filler. Sand surfaces with medium coarse 80-grit glass paper, followed by a light sanding with 120-grit. Open-grained veneers, such as oak or walnut, must be filled and re-sanded; close-grained hardwoods such as beech need not be filled. Wood filler must match the wood colour if you want to use a clear finish; if staining the wood first, a neutral paste is required.

The edges of manufactured board should be trimmed with veneer tape. Alternatively, a rounded wooden edge called a nosing, or square wooden lipping, can be fixed with PVA glue and panel pins. Plywood edges may be left uncovered, but will need to be filled with wood filler and sanded smooth.

Worktop surfaces are generally applied after the cabinet is installed. For some surfaces you must prepare the worktop in advance. Plastic laminate, the most common, requires a built-up edge on an unfinished manufactured board worktop *(page 29,* *Step 1, inset)*. Worktops can now be bought cut to your own specifications and with a curved edge. Ends are unfinished but edging strip is supplied.

Marble or slate worktops, generally 20 mm thick, are more elegant—and more expensive. In this thickness, stone does not need a specially prepared worktop; a commercial dealer (listed under "Marble Services" in the Yellow Pages) will cut each piece to your specifications.

If you use 13 mm slate rather than the more expensive 20 mm material, install a plywood worktop and cover its exposed edges with 28 mm hardwood lipping *(page 29, Step 2)* set flush with the bottom of the worktop and protruding above the top.

Stone worktops are heavy—up to 9 kilograms per 300 mm—and fragile; get helpers to support the slab at 1-metre intervals, to prevent it from breaking of its own weight.

A Range of Coatings

Material	Characteristics	Limitations	Comments
Paint, oil-modified alkyd	Flexible and durable; resists moisture and stains; opaque, available in all colours and finishes, from matt to high-gloss; hides imperfections in wood and construction	Primer must be used; disagreeable fumes when wet	High-gloss finish is most durable. Recommended for use on less expensive woods with unattractive grain
Paint, single-pack polyurethane or epoxy resin	Used like alkyd paints; have great resistance to water, alkalis and wear	Primer must be used	Expensive
Stain, oil-based penetrating	Does not raise the grain; rich tone; easier to use than water-based stains; must be covered by varnish	Soaks into soft woods producing striped effect; hard to remove	Suitable for coarse-grained woods such as mahogany
Stain, oil-based non-penetrating	Disguises cheap woods and makes different woods look uniform; lightens coarse-grained woods and tones down grain with uneven colour distribution; must be covered by varnish	Darkens soft, porous wood; does not take well on hardwoods	Must be pre-mixed if using more than one tin to get even colour; suitable for close-grained woods
Stain, water-based, penetrating	Sold as a powder that is mixed with water; penetrates wood deeply and is available in wide range of colours; must be covered by varnish	Raises the grain of the wood so that the surface must be sanded repeatedly	A frequent choice despite difficulties of use because of its colour qualities; suitable for all woods; inexpensive
Varnish, urethane	Clear finish; applied in at least two coats (sand between coats); water, stain and scratch-resistant; gloss or matt finish	Difficult to recoat	Also known as polyurethane; oil-based type discolours least and high-gloss is most durable; recommended for clear-finished interior built-ins

Choosing a wood finish. The paints, stains and varnishes best suited for finishing the wood of built-ins are described in this chart. All are quite tough and some, such as urethane varnish and high-quality gloss paint, can substitute for worktops if great resistance to moisture and cleaning compounds is not essential. Emulsion paints are not listed because of their limited durability and because water-based paints swell the particles of wood chipboard, giving a textured finish. They can be used on other manufactured boards where they will not be exposed to heavy use.

Worktop Surfaces

Material	Characteristics	Limitations	Comments
SYNTHETICS			
Plastic laminate	Inexpensive and available in a wide range of colours, patterns and textures, including imitation marble, slate and wood grain; pieces are cut to size with a scoring tool from sheets measuring 1220 by 2440, 2740 or 3050 mm, and fastened with a contact adhesive; edges are finished with a router; exceptionally tough, resisting most stains and scratches	Edges can chip and surface can be damaged by sharp knives; sheets peel away if water seeps beneath them; scorched by cigarettes and very hot cooking pans	Most commonly used worktop; recommended for all applications where appearance is acceptable
Ceramic tile	Beautifully smooth and shiny or frosted surface; available in many colours and designs either singly or in kits containing specially shaped edging tiles that prevent water running off the front edge; mosaic tiles are sold attached to sheets of paper or a mesh backing, and are set on to adhesive and grouted in; ordinarily 6 mm thick in square or rectangular shapes, 25 to 300 mm in size; almost totally water and heat-resistant	Can chip, scratch or crack; grout between tiles stains easily; hard surface makes kitchenware clatter and can cause breakages	Stains can be removed with diluted bleach; coloured grout helps disguise stains; not the most practical surface for kitchens or bathrooms
Acrylic-resin sheets ("synthetic marble")	Often called Corian, a trade name; available in almond, beige and white through builders' merchants; looks much like marble; can be cut with a power saw and shaped with a router; resists moisture, stains, heat and cracks; ordinarily 6 mm thick	Limited range of colours; scratches easily; costly	Scratches and scorches can be sanded out
STONES			
Granite	Strong and impervious to heat, moisture and stains; takes a bright polish; available in many colours; ordinarily 20 mm thick	More expensive than the other stones; very heavy; hard	Most suitable of the stones for kitchens and bathrooms
Marble	Porous and brittle; available in a wide range of colours; takes a bright polish; ordinarily 20 mm thick	Scratches easily and can crack or break if heavy object is dropped on it; readily attacked by acids such as vinegar and lemon; easily stained, even by water	Wax sealer can be used to improve stain resistance; professionals can repair cracks and scratches; especially suitable for formal rooms
Slate	Heat-resistant; available in green, blue and grey; takes a good natural polish but doesn't retain it well; ordinarily 20 mm thick	Scratches easily; oil and grease difficult to remove	Can be waxed or varnished but varnish difficult to renew; often used as a thin 13 mm veneer over a hidden plywood top *(opposite, above, and page 45)*

Choosing a worktop. The headings in this chart are identical to those in the chart on the opposite page, but the materials in the first column are grouped in two categories: the first group consists of synthetic worktop surfaces, and the second group consists of worktops that are made of natural stone. All these materials offer a variety of textures and colours that add elegance to a built-in and to the room it fits into. All provide much greater resistance to moisture, heat and stains than finished wood, and they are used not only to top kitchen cabinets, bathroom counters and bars but also for parts of shelves and bookcases that might be resting places for ashtrays or drink glasses.

Installing a
Solid Stone Worktop

1 Applying adhesive. With a caulking gun apply 25 mm beads of neoprene adhesive to the strips at the top of the carcass, running the beads about 35 mm from the front and back edges. Wipe the bottom side of the stone slab clean and, with one helper for every metre of stone, lift it over the cabinet. Set the back edge on the cabinet, tight against the wall, then slowly lower the front edge on to the frame.

If you cannot find a neoprene adhesive in your local shop, use a two-part epoxy resin suitable for bonding stone to wood and follow the manufacturer's instructions carefully.

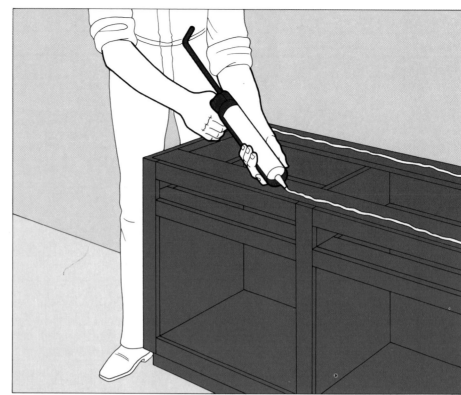

2 Adjusting the overhang. Hold a wood block 25 mm thick flat against the carcass just beneath the stone top, and use the block as a gauge to check the overhang of the stone top. Get a helper to adjust the top by pushing it until the overhang is even on all exposed sides; wipe off any excess adhesive at once with a wet rag.

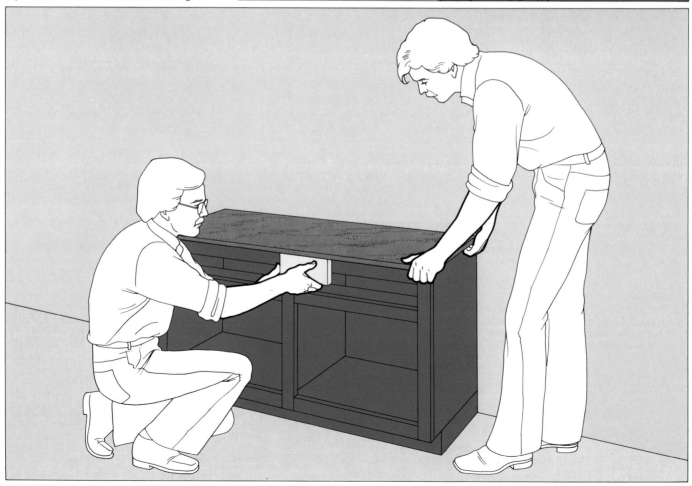

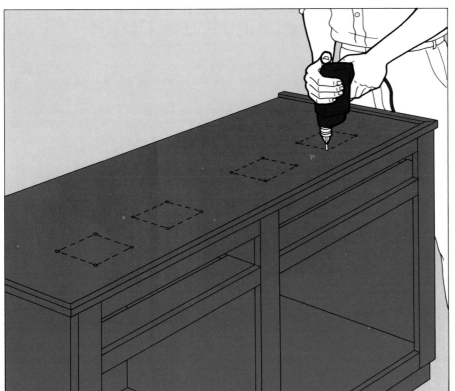

Setting a Slate Slab on a Wooden Worktop

1 **Preparing the worktop.** In a worktop edged with 30 mm lipping *(page 29, Step 2)*, saw four access holes, each about 150 mm square, by drilling holes at the corners and cutting out the squares with a jigsaw. Locate them about 200 mm from the front of the cabinet and space them to avoid any cabinet partitions.

2 **Lowering the stone.** After applying adhesive to the edges of the worktop, lay three or four scraps of wood across the worktop lipping, resting their inner ends on the worktop, and get at least two helpers to assist you in handling the stone. With one helper at each end of the cabinet and the third reaching up through one pair of access holes, gently lower the slate slab on to the worktop, resting the front edge of the slab on the scrap wood pieces. Slide the slab tight against the walls at the back or side of the cabinet. Now get the two helpers to raise the slab slightly through the access holes while you remove the wood scraps; finally, the helpers at the access holes should gently lower the slab to the worktop.

Anchoring a Cabinet to the Structure of the House

Like any other built-in, a cabinet must be fastened to a house. Wall cabinets are fixed to the brick or blockwork of a solid wall, or to the studs within a plasterboard partition wall; ceiling cabinets hang from the joists or concrete above the ceilings. Even floor cabinets are fastened to the floor and to a wall if they stand against one.

When planning the position of your cabinet, make certain no services run where it will be secured to the wall or floor, and avoid hanging a heavy cabinet on a plasterboard stud partition wall. Locate the joists and studs by lightly tapping the ceiling or wall surface in a straight line, until the tone differs. Drive a long panel pin through the surface to check that you have correctly located the joist or stud. Tap the surface again at 400, 450 or 600 mm centres to locate the next joists or studs.

Mark off the cabinet location by drawing lines on the wall or ceiling or, to avoid marring paint or panelling, by running strips of masking tape. For a wall cabinet, you will need a horizontal line for the bottom of the cabinet (this line is normally 1500 to 1600 mm above the floor or 450 mm above a worktop) and a vertical line for one side. If possible, align the top of the cabinet with door and window architraves. On stud walls, mark the centre of each stud above and below the installation area.

For ceiling cabinets, use the hanging frame (page 55, centre) as a template to outline the installation area; for floor cabinets, use the base frame. Floor cabinets can be installed over any flooring; if the room is carpeted set the base frame in place, cut the carpet along the edges of the frame with a trimming knife, then remove that section of the carpet.

Placing a cabinet in a wall recess is trickier. Because walls and ceilings are rarely completely flat, a wall cabinet should be about 6 mm narrower than the recess; the gaps between the cabinet and the walls can be covered with moulding. A cabinet that rises to the ceiling should be set about 19 mm below the ceiling. To allow for the moulding that will cover the gap between cabinet and ceiling, build a cabinet so that its front will be set back at least 50 mm from the front corners of the recess.

For the installation itself, nail a horizontal 75 by 25 mm to the wall as a temporary ledger (below) to support a wall cabinet and keep it level. For a heavy cabinet or a set of cabinets, place vertical 100 by 50 mm props between the cabinet bottom and the floor. Remove the skirting board before installing a base cabinet; later on, cut it so that it will fit against the edges of the installed cabinet. If the hinges of the cabinet doors have removable pins, take the doors off before starting the job. And recruit enough helpers to hold cabinets steady as you drill pilot holes and drive in screws.

In joists and studs, use No. 8 black Japan round-head screws at least 62 mm long so that they will run 25 mm into the supporting joist or stud. In masonry walls use plastic plugs that fit into drilled holes in the wall, and No. 10 screws, 67 to 75 mm long, that pass through the cabinet and into the plugs. Secure cabinets to the wall top and bottom. The wall cabinets in this chapter are built with hanging rails (page 16), which strengthen a unit at the top, where it is most liable to pull away from the wall.

On a plaster wall, you can sand away the small bumps that prevent a cabinet from fitting snugly and hanging plumb, but for larger wall irregularities—particularly in plasterboard—it is easier to alter the cabinet. A well-built cabinet has a face frame and 13 mm scribing strips (page 16); the frame and strips can be planed to fit against most bumps and depressions. The strips protrude past the back of a cabinet, creating a gap between the back panel of the cabinet and the wall; use shims to fill this gap and to plumb a cabinet.

To complete an installation, cover the gaps between the cabinet and the wall and ceiling. Many moulding styles are available; in the examples illustrated on these pages, a right-angled scotia moulding is used to cover a gap of up to 12 mm between a cabinet and a wall; a 50 mm coving covers a similar gap between a cabinet top and a ceiling. To cover a larger gap—as much as 150 mm—between a cabinet and the ceiling, use a fascia made of plywood, of wood matching the cabinet, or of painted or papered plasterboard.

Hanging a Wall Cabinet

1 **Installing a temporary ledger.** Set a 75 by 25 cut to the width of the cabinet flat against the wall, with its top at the line that marks the cabinet bottom. Nail the board to the wall—at each stud it crosses if it is a partition wall; let the nail heads protrude 6 mm. Check the board to be sure it is level; if it is not, remove enough nails to reset it.

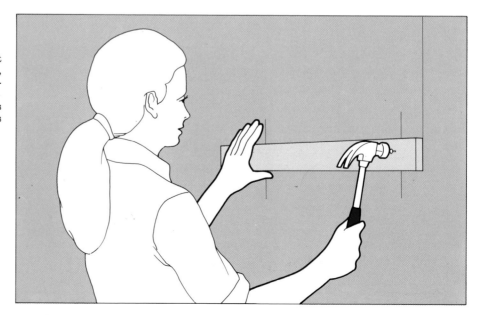

2 **Shimming the top of the cabinet.** Set the back of the cabinet on the ledger and align the side with the vertical mark you have made on the wall, then ask a helper to hold the cabinet against the wall while you use a level to check the face for plumb. If the top of the cabinet must move out from the wall, shim it out at each corner, or if the wall is a stud wall insert a shim at each stud, far enough to move the cabinet top the required distance. If the cabinet must move out at the bottom, use shims at the top only to fill the gap between the back and the wall; tap them into place without moving the cabinet.

In a wall recess where you cannot reach over the top of a cabinet to insert shims, nail a 19 mm wood strip to the top of the cabinet back between the scribing strips, and shim the bottom of the cabinet *(Step 3, below)* to make it plumb. In either case, proceed immediately to Step 3.

Hiding Gaps with Moulding

3 **Fastening the cabinet to the wall.** Drill pilot holes through the hanging rail, cabinet back and shims, and into the brick, block or studs; then screw the top of the cabinet to the wall with 75 mm No. 8 screws, using plugs in masonry. Remove the ledger and shim the cabinet bottom at each corner or stud, filling the gap between the back and the wall and, if necessary, plumbing the cabinet. While your helper presses the cabinet against the bottom shims, drill and drive screws through the cabinet back and through these shims into the wall.

Trim protruding shim ends with a handsaw: cut almost to the wall, then snap off the waste.

At the sides of a cabinet. Cut two strips of 19 mm scotia moulding to the height of the cabinet and cut the bottom end of each strip to a line that reverses the contour of the moulding *(inset)*. Set the flat sides of the mouldings in the angle formed by the cabinet and the wall. Fasten each strip to the cabinet with panel pins spaced 150 mm apart.

Round a recessed wall cabinet. Cut a strip of 50 mm coving to the width of the recess, hold it in place against the ceiling and the face of the cabinet and trace its bottom edge across the cabinet; then nail a 25 by 19 mm nailing strip of the same length flat against the cabinet, with its bottom at the traced line. Set the bottom of the coving flush with the bottom of the nailing strip and nail the coving to the strip.

Cut a strip of 19 mm scotia moulding to the width of the recess, mitre the ends to a 45-degree angle and nail the moulding to the cabinet directly beneath the nailing strip. Then cut two strips of scotia moulding to match the height of the cabinet; mitre the top of each strip to fit the top strip and cut the bottom of each by the method shown on page 47, bottom right; nail the strips to the sides of the cabinet face frame *(inset)*.

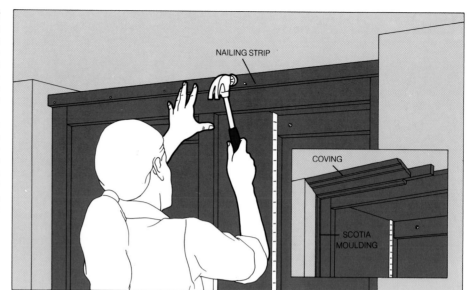

Scribing and Shaping for a Perfect Fit

Marking the scribing strips. Run masking tape along the outside of each scribing strip, ask a helper to hold the cabinet on a temporary ledger and shim the back to make the cabinet plumb *(page 47, Step 2)*; if the cabinet must be shimmed at the bottom, use props *(opposite page, Step 2)* rather than a ledger to help support the cabinet. Set the legs of a pair of compasses 6 mm apart, place the pivot point against the wall and put the pencil at the top of a scribing strip; run the compasses down the wall. Plane each strip down to the pencilled line. It may be necessary to set the cabinet back in position, then take it down and plane it, several times for a precise fit.

Remove the tapes and hang the cabinet *(page 47, Step 3)*, shimming at the corners or studs to fill gaps between the cabinet and the wall.

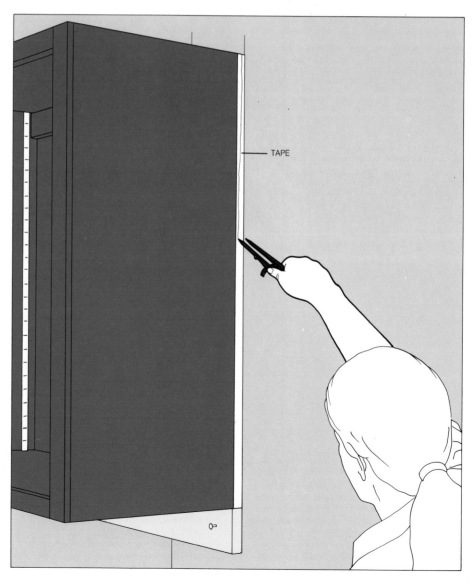

Hanging a Set of Cabinets

1 **Linking the cabinets together.** Set the cabinets side by side on the floor, face up, and clamp adjacent sides together with G-cramps; protect the cabinets with scraps of softwood between the jaws of each cramp. Drill pilot holes about 100 mm from the top and bottom and 75 mm in from the front and back, and screw the cabinets together with 32 mm No. 6 countersunk screws.

If the face frames will be overlapped by doors, drill pilot holes level with the fastening screws, from the inside edge of each frame into the adjacent frame and drive 75 mm No. 8 screws into the holes. Finally, sand all the face frames to make them completely flush with each other.

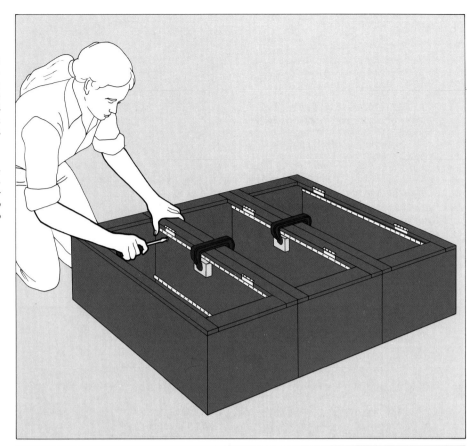

2 **Propping the cabinets against the wall.** Install a temporary ledger *(page 46, Step 1)* for the row of cabinets and, with two or more helpers, raise the cabinets on to the ledger; for additional support, position 100 by 50 mm props at the sides and middle of the cabinet row. Get the helpers to hold the cabinets while you plumb and hang the entire set as a single unit.

A Fascia for a Ceiling Gap

1 Marking the ceiling. At 125 mm intervals, set the edge of a ruler against the sides and the face frames with the end of the ruler touching the ceiling, and mark the ceiling at the back edge of the ruler. Connect the marks with solid lines then, for a ceiling with joists, tap the ceiling to determine the location and direction of the joists. If the joists are perpendicular to the cabinet faces, as in the example shown here, mark the location of each joist on the line above the front of the cabinets. If they are parallel to the cabinets and there is no joist directly above the line, proceed directly to Step 2, below.

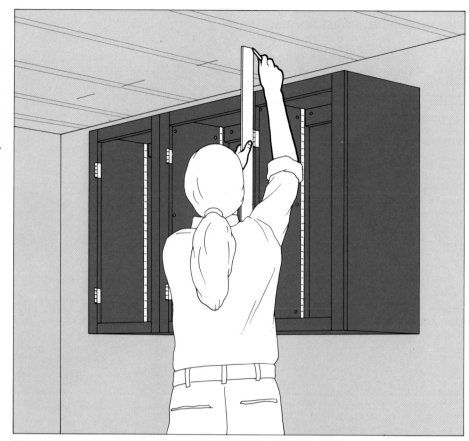

2 Installing the cleats. Cut a 50 by 25 mm cleat to the length of the front line on the ceiling and side cleats to fit between the front cleat and the wall, and fasten the cleats to the ceiling with their front edges directly within the lines. If the joists are perpendicular to the cabinets, nail the front cleat to each joist it crosses. If there is no joist directly above a front or side cleat, use toggle bolts *(inset)* to fasten the cleat directly to the ceiling.

Drill holes through the cleats and the ceiling board at 150 mm intervals, and run the bolts through the holes in the cleat. Remove the bolts, screw the toggles on to the bolts, and then push the toggles through the holes in the ceiling. As you tighten each bolt, the toggles will open and pull the cleat to the ceiling.

For a concrete ceiling, drill and plug pilot holes at 300 mm intervals and secure the cleats using 50 mm No. 8 screws.

Cut fascia boards 19 mm thick, long enough to cover the gaps above the cabinets and wide enough to overlap the face frames and sides by 12 mm. Cut 45-degree bevels on the ends that will form corners.

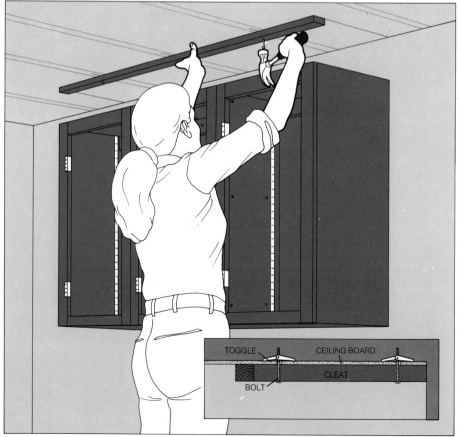

3 Fastening the fascia. At 150 mm intervals, nail the bottoms of the fascia boards to the cabinets and the tops to the cleats. At each corner, fasten the boards together with a single panel pin.

If a cleat is fastened to the ceiling with toggle bolts rather than nails, drill pilot holes and fasten the fascia board to the cleat with 37 mm No. 6 screws—the force of a hammer blow could rip the toggle-bolted cleat off the ceiling.

4 Covering the ceiling joint. Set a strip of coving against the ceiling and the front fascia board, and mark the bottom edge of the coving at the ends of the board; mark the side covings to fit between the front of the fascia and the wall. For each corner, place the covings upside down in a mitre box, with the angled surfaces against the fence and bottom of the box. Set the saw to a 45-degree angle and cut the piece for the left side of the corner with the saw handle to the left *(inset)*, and the piece for the right side of the corner with the handle to the right. Nail the covings to the fascia boards at 150 mm intervals.

LEFT SIDE CORNER

5 Covering the cabinet joint. Cut strips of 16 mm scotia moulding to the length and width of the cabinets and make 45-degree mitre cuts at the ends that will form exterior corners; then set each strip flush with the bottom edge of a fascia board and nail the strip to the cabinet every 150 mm.

If your fascia consists of plasterboard covered with wallpaper, choose a scotia moulding slightly wider than the bottom edge of the fascia, to conceal the exposed edge of the wallpaper.

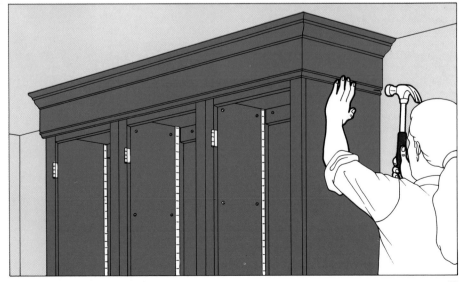

Mounting a Base Cabinet

1 **Levelling the base.** Set the base in position and tap shims under one or more corners to level it; tap additional shims at the front of the base under each bearer to fill any gaps between the base and floor. For a base that stands against a stud wall, mark the positions of studs along its rear edge and at the height of the cabinet top.

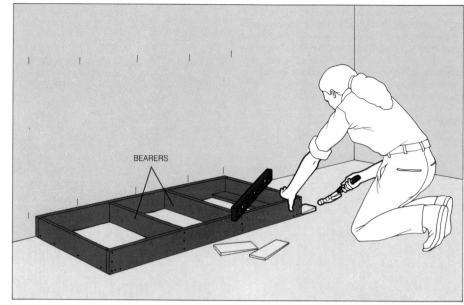

BEARERS

2 **Fastening the base.** At each corner of the base, drill a pilot hole and drive a 63 mm No. 8 screw through the screwing strip, the shim and the floor. At each bearer, toenail through the base, shim and floor. Trim the ends of the shims as described on page 47, Step 3.

An island-cabinet base *(inset)* has extra 100 by 25 mm screwing strips at the bottom and 50 by 25 mm strips at the top: screw the base down at three points along each bottom strip, and mark the base front at the centre of each top strip.

Cover the exposed sides of the base and shims with vinyl skirting or 6 mm exterior quality plywood boards cut 6 mm wider than the base sides and scribed and planed so that the bottom edge fits the floor and the top edge rests about 6 mm below the top of the base side. Fasten the plywood with 25 mm panel pins.

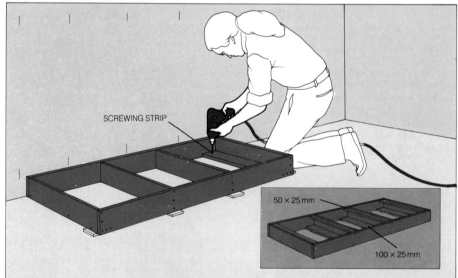

SCREWING STRIP

50 × 25 mm

100 × 25 mm

3 **Fastening the cabinet to the base.** Set the cabinet with its back against the wall and its sides and front overlapping the base frame by 75 mm. Scribe the back of the cabinet if necessary *(page 48)*. Inside the cabinet measure 75 mm in from each side and drive 50 mm lost-head nails at 150 mm intervals through the cabinet bottom into the sides of the frame.

On an island cabinet, use 37 mm No. 8 screws rather than nails and fasten the bottom at three points along each top screwing strip, lining the screws up with the marks made at the top of the base front in Step 2.

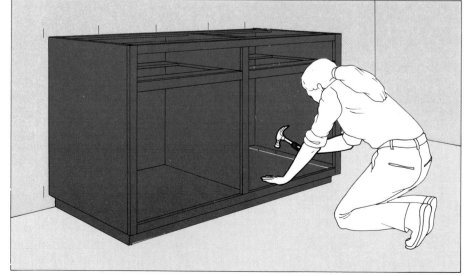

4 **Screwing a cabinet to the wall.** Shim the cabinet to fill any gaps, either at each stud position or, on a masonry wall, 150 mm from each corner plus one shim in the centre. Drill pilot holes through the cabinet back, the shim and into the wall, and insert plugs in masonry. Fix the cabinet to the wall using 62 mm No. 8 screws. Trim the protruding shim ends.

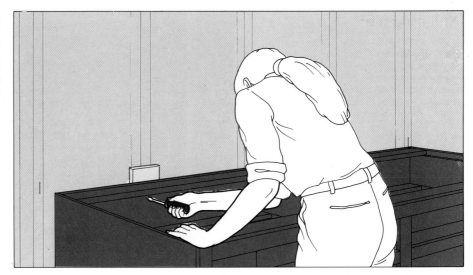

Fitting a Cabinet Top to an Alcove

1 **Making a template.** Cut two pieces of 3 mm hardboard, long enough to overlap when fitted into the alcove and wide enough to overhang the front of the cabinet by 50 mm. Set the pieces on the cabinet, push them into the corners and, using a pair of compasses with the legs set slightly wider than the widest gap between the wall and the hardboard, scribe the contours of the side and back walls on both pieces of hardboard. Remove the hardboard, and plane or saw the edges of both pieces to the pencil lines. Replace both halves of the template against the corners of the alcove and tack them together at their overlap. Across the front of the template, draw a guideline 25 mm out from the front of the cabinet frame.

2 **Marking the cabinet top.** Remove the template from the cabinet and clamp it to the finished side of the cabinet top, with the guideline on the template flush with the front of the top, and draw the outline of the template on the top. Remove the template and cut the edges of the cabinet top with a handsaw, then plane them smooth.

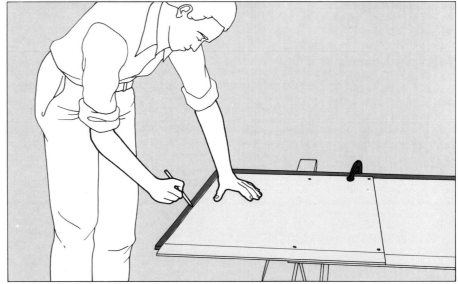

3 **Fastening the cabinet top.** Set the cabinet top in place flush with the alcove walls, drill pilot holes up through the cabinet screwing strips and drive 32 mm No. 8 screws into the cabinet top at 150 mm intervals. Get a helper to hold down the top while you secure the screws. Cover the exposed edge of the cabinet top with wooden lipping *(page 29, Step 2)*.

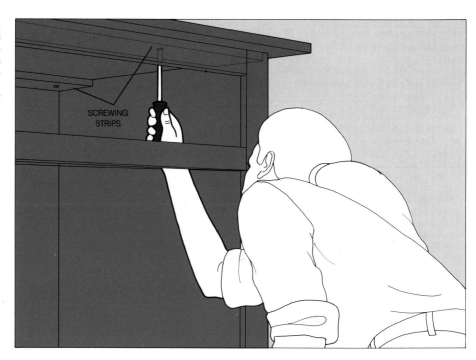

Stacking a Two-Piece Unit

A bookcase on a base cabinet. Set in place the upper half of the unit—in this example, a bookcase assembled with hanging rails but without a base *(page 19)*—and outline the bottoms of the stiles on the cabinet top. Remove the bookcase, drill a pilot hole down through the cabinet top at the centre of each stile position, then replace the bookcase and drive 50 mm No. 8 screws up through the top into each stile. Shim the back of the bookcase *(page 47, Step 2)*, drill pilot holes through the hanging rails and screw the bookcase to the wall. Nail coving directly to the face frame to conceal the gaps between the top of the unit and the ceiling.

Installing a Floor-to-Ceiling Unit

1 **Raising the unit.** After installing a base *(page 52, Steps 1–2)*, set the unit—here, a bookcase—face down on the floor and, with a helper, swing it upwards on its lower edge until it stands upright in front of the base.

2 **Fastening the unit in place.** With a helper, set the unit on the base and against the wall, with the front and sides of the unit overlapping the base by 75 mm. Nail the unit bottom to the base *(page 52, Step 3)*, then shim the top and drive screws through the hanging rail into the wall. Use coving *(page 51, Steps 4–5)* to hide the gaps between the unit top and the ceiling.

For a unit installed as a room divider, with one side against a wall, build a base with extra screwing strips *(page 52, Step 2, inset)*. Use the same base for a unit that has no wall support, and fasten the unit to the ceiling. Install a 19 mm filler strip, shimmed flush with the ceiling, between the unit and the ceiling, and drive 87 mm No. 10 screws through the unit top and the filler strip into the joist or joists above. If you are fixing to a concrete ceiling, drill and plug pilot holes before installing the unit.

Hanging Room-Divider Cabinets from the Ceiling

1 **A hanging frame for a ceiling unit.** The outside of this frame consists of 18 mm boards 150 mm wide, cut to the length and width of the cabinets that will hang from it, and butt-nailed at the corners. Upper and lower crosspieces are screwed in place through the outside of the frame. The upper crosspieces are 100 by 50s spaced at equal intervals and, when fixed to a ceiling with joists, set at right angles to the overhead joists; they are shimmed at the joist positions to make the frame level and fastened to the joists with 87 mm No. 10 screws. For a concrete ceiling use plugged 80 mm No. 5 screws. The lower crosspieces—100 by 50s at the front and back, and a 150 by 50 in the middle—are positioned over the hanging rails *(Step 2, below)*.

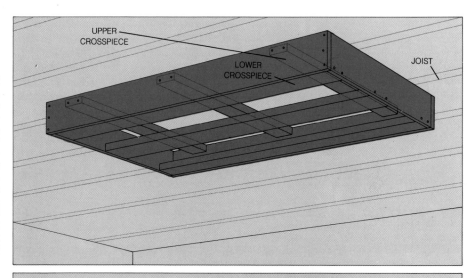

2 **Fastening the cabinets to the frame.** After fastening a row of cabinets together *(page 49, Step 1)*, attach hanging rails *(page 27)* inside the tops of each cabinet at front and back, corresponding with the positions of the lower crosspieces on the ceiling frame, and then get helpers to hold the cabinets up against the frame while you drill pilot holes. Locate these screwholes at the left and right ends of all the hanging rails and screw the cabinets to the crosspieces with 62 mm No. 8 screws. Fasten each back-to-back pair of cabinets together with two 9 mm No. 6 screws and cover the joints at the ceiling and the bottom of the hanging frame with mouldings.

55

Cabinets that Blend an Appliance into a Room

A custom-built cabinet can make an appliance or fixture more attractive—and more useful. More attractive, because the cabinet either covers or camouflages a bulky machine and blends with the room's decor. More useful, because the cabinet provides storage above or below.

Kitchen appliances make particularly good candidates for this treatment. In fact, some are designed specifically to fit into the standard array of kitchen units. A dishwasher matches the height and depth of a row of base units and fits directly underneath a worktop; a hob must be fitted into a hole in a worktop; many refrigerators and hob extractor fans are factory-fitted with face panels to which fronts matching the kitchen units can be fixed.

Both a standard refrigerator and an eye-level oven must have specialized cabinets round them for a built-in effect. Any modern refrigerator that has bottom-mounted coils is easily enclosed in a cabinet (page 58) that frames the front of the appliance and provides a storage area above. A refrigerator with back-mounted coils needs more clearance for ventilation—follow the manufacturer's recommendations for the cabinet dimensions. An oven cabinet (page 58) provides storage space above and below, and also supports the oven.

Make the top for a refrigerator or oven cabinet level with adjacent cabinet tops; if space between the adjacent cabinets and the ceiling is covered by a fascia or coving, use the same over the appliance cabinet.

Because either a refrigerator or oven cabinet may be taller and wider than a standard doorway, plan to assemble them in the kitchen. If you design either of them to reach all the way to the ceiling, make the diagonal measurements of the cabinet sides 25 mm less than the height of the room (page 59); whatever the depth of the sides, this limitation will permit you to tilt the cabinet to an upright position without hitting the ceiling.

A smaller, easier-to-build cabinet—for a fixture rather than an appliance—is the radiator cover illustrated on these pages. This cover is little more than a box that fits over the radiator and against the wall, and has perforated aluminium sheeting tacked to a front frame.

Since any cover cuts a radiator's efficiency, choose a sheeting with a pattern of large holes or openings, to allow as much air flow as possible. In addition, tack aluminium foil to the underside of the top and, if possible, to the wall behind the radiator—it will increase efficiency by reflecting heat. Aluminium sheeting and foil are available at hardware shops and builders' merchants. Vary the design of a radiator cabinet to suit your requirements: you can, for example, cut an opening in the top for an inset of perforated aluminium sheeting, or hinge a small section of the top or side for easy access to the nipples or valves.

The techniques for building cabinets for large appliances are those described earlier in this chapter, slightly modified for each appliance. Oven cabinets should be assembled with screws rather than nails for greater strength. Refrigerator and oven cabinets should be stained or painted in place; radiator covers can be finished before they are installed.

A Cover for a Radiator

1 **Making the face frame.** Glue and butt-nail two horizontal rails between two vertical stiles. Make the assembly from 50 by 19 mm timber, with the stiles cut 75 mm longer than the height of the radiator, and the rails 50 mm longer than the total width of the radiator and valve. Set the first rail between the tops of the stiles and the second at least 75 mm from the floor for proper air flow; if the bottom of the radiator is less than 75 mm above the floor, position the rail to leave the radiator partially exposed.

With the frame face down, nail perforated aluminium sheeting over the framed opening.

2 **Attaching the sides and brace.** Nail the stiles to the front edges of 18 mm sides, which are cut to the height of the stiles and 38 mm wider than the depth of the radiator from the wall. Fasten a 100 by 25 mm brace across the interior of the cover, flush with the top and 12 mm in from the back, using four nails driven through the sides and into the ends of the brace.

Cut an 18 mm top 50 mm wider and 25 mm deeper than the unit. Finish the front and side edges and tack plain aluminium foil to the underside of the top.

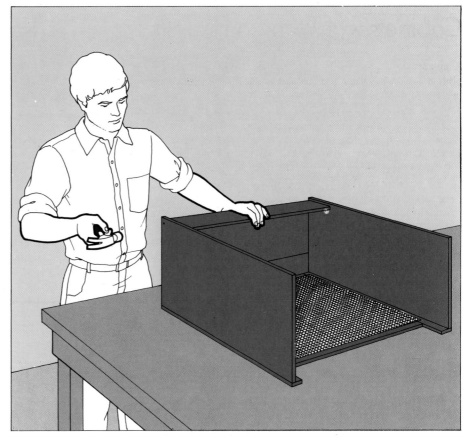

3 **Attaching the top.** Set the back of the top flush with the back edges of the sides. Fasten the top in place with nails or panel pins driven every 200 mm into the sides, front rail and back brace.

Cut 50 by 25 mm cleats to the height of the sides, and attach them to the wall: use plugged screws in masonry; on a stud wall use nails or, if the cleat does not line up with a stud, fasten it to the plasterboard with toggle bolts. Locate the cleats just inside the points where the sides of the cover will fit. After scribing and shaping the sides of the cover to fit the wall and skirting board *(page 48)*, screw the unit to each cleat.

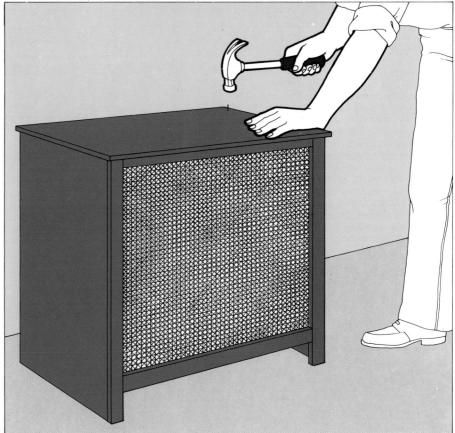

Building in
Large Kitchen Appliances

A built-in refrigerator. This enclosure is essentially a top cabinet *(page 16)*. Cut each of the sides to the distance between the back of the refrigerator-door gasket and the wall, and to the height of the adjacent cabinet tops; if adjacent cabinets reach the ceiling, cut each side so that its diagonal measurement equals the height of the room less 25 mm *(opposite page, Step 1)*.

Cut a top and shelf to the width of the refrigerator plus 125 mm. In each side, cut a rebate for the top and a housing that will set the shelf at the level above the top of the refrigerator recommended by the manufacturer. Then cut a back to fit the space between the shelf and the top, add a hanging rail *(page 27, Step 4)* and cut a rebate in each side to hold the back. Glue and nail the pieces together *(pages 26–29)*.

Use 50 by 19 planed-all-round timber for the stiles and rails of the face frame. Install doors *(pages 37–41)* on the section of the cabinet above the refrigerator. Then fasten 38 by 19 mm cleats to the inside bottoms of both sides, and drive nails through the cleats into the floor. Fasten the top of the cabinet to the wall by nailing through the hanging rail; in a stud wall, nail into the studs.

A built-in wall oven. This floor-to-ceiling cabinet combines features of base and wall-mounted cabinets. The sides are 50 mm deeper than the oven, with diagonal measurements that match the height of the room less 25 mm *(opposite page, Step 1)*. The back is the same height as the sides, and as wide as the oven plus 125 mm, with a hanging rail fastened across the top and a hole for the oven's electric socket cut at the location specified by the manufacturer.

Inside the cabinet a top, a bottom and an intermediate shelf fit into the sides: the bottom fits into housings 32 mm above the bottom edges, the shelf into housings 12 mm above the top of the oven, and the top into rebates cut across the top edges. Rebates along the back edges of the sides receive the back of the cabinet. The face frame is made of 50 by 19 mm timber except for the rail beneath the oven, which is 100 by 19 mm timber. The entire cabinet rests on a base 130 mm high.

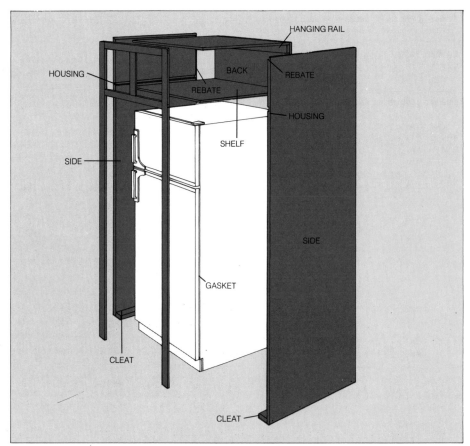

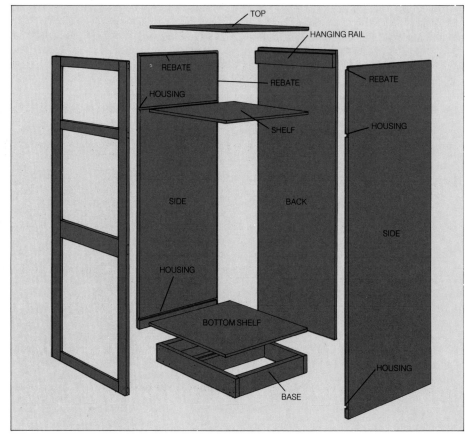

Making an Oven Cabinet

1 **Measuring and cutting the sides.** Mark the depth of a side along the top edge of a panel and get a helper to hold the end of a steel tape measure at the mark. Extend the tape to the height of the room less 25 mm, swing the tape to the side of the panel and mark the point where the tape meets the side edge. From this mark, measure and mark the depth of the side, then connect all the marks and cut the side. Cut the second side, cut the remaining pieces as shown in the anatomy *(opposite page, below)* and assemble the cabinet by the methods indicated on pages 26–29.

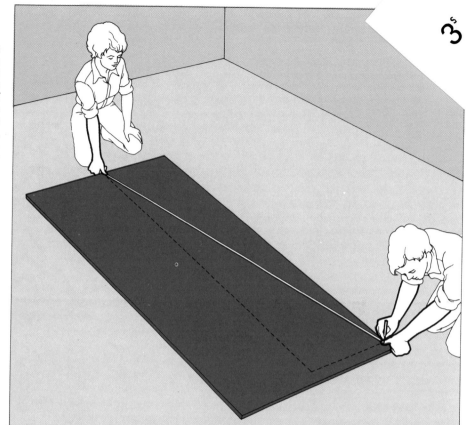

2 **Making the face frame.** Glue and butt-nail four rails between two stiles. Start this part of the job by cutting stiles of 50 by 19 mm timber to the height of the cabinet. Cut the rails to the width of the oven plus 125 mm. Make three rails of 50 by 19 mm timber, the first to go between the tops of the stiles, the second between the bottoms, and the third 12 mm above the top of the oven opening. Drill two pilot holes through the stiles at the position of each rail and use 63 mm No. 8 screws to secure the stiles and rails together. Cut the fourth rail of 100 by 19 mm timber, and fasten it at the bottom of the oven opening. Attach the face frame to the cabinet *(page 33, Step 7)*.

Cut two 100 by 50 supports to the depth of the cabinet sides; the oven will rest on these supports.

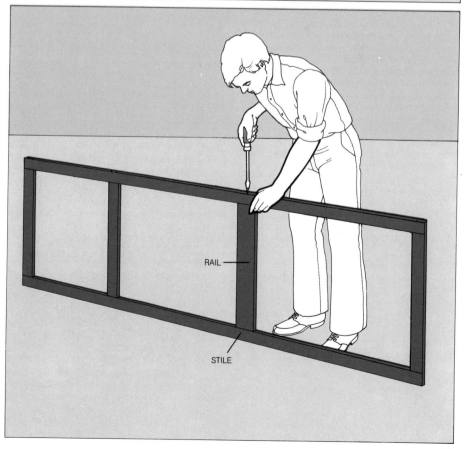

RAIL

STILE

rewing in the oven supports. Hold a support
at inside the cabinet from front to back, with its
upper corner against an upper corner of the rail
at the bottom of the oven opening and mark its
position on the rail. Drill two pilot holes through
the rail and two through the cabinet back. Secure
the rail and the back to the ends of the support
with 50 mm No. 8 screws. Attach the second support on the other side of the cabinet in the same
way. Then cut two 75 by 25 mm cleats to the inside width of the cabinet.

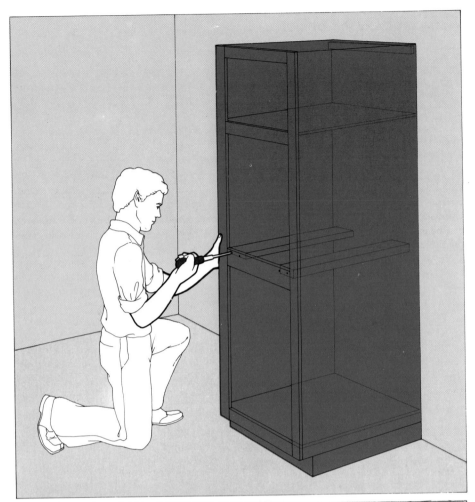

4 Installing cleats for extra strength. Hold a cleat
inside the cabinet with its ends against the sides,
its face against the bottoms of the supports and
its edge against the front rail. Drill pilot holes
through each cabinet side and use two 50 mm
No. 8 screws to secure the sides to the ends of the
cleat. Attach the second cleat under the 100 by
50 mm supports at the back of the cabinet.

Install doors above the oven opening and either
doors or drawers below *(pages 34–41)*; fasten the
cabinet to its base *(page 52, Steps 1–3)* and to the
wall behind it, screwing into the studs if it is a
stud wall *(page 47, Steps 2–3)*.

Wall-to-Wall Storage

The ultimate in built-in cabinetry is the storage wall, created by building vertical partitions out from one wall in a room and then filling the space between them with shelves, drawers or clothes rails.

The timber frame shown on these pages makes a simple but versatile skeleton for such a storage wall. The entire structure, which is made of any of the manufactured boards—that is, plywood, blockboard, or chipboard—preferably 16 to 18 mm thick, can be cut with a circular or table saw. Its partitions can be placed for convenience anywhere between side walls; normally the partitions are ceiling-high, but some are shorter to accommodate a long shelf above. Convenience also determines how far they protrude from the old wall, but a depth of 600 mm permits two partitions to be cut from a standard 2440 by 1220 mm board. This depth is sufficient to allow standard clothes hangers to hang freely, and will house large items such as a television or music centre. The partitions are fixed to the frame, their bottoms extend over a floor plinth and a fascia across their tops hides the joins with the ceiling. Use nails to secure plywood and blockboard, and chipboard screws for chipboard.

Clothes rails (made from either metal tubing or 25 mm wooden dowelling) or shelves can span any interval between partitions but both need intermediate support brackets at least every 800 mm. At the partitions, clothes rails are best supported by special end brackets available from hardware shops.

Install shelves using standards for adjustable shelves *(page 11)*, and cleats *(page 102)* or jointing blocks *(pages 9–10)* for permanent shelves. If you are using jointing blocks, get a helper to hold the shelves in position on the pre-installed partitions while you secure the blocks. Position drawers *(pages 34–36)* and doors *(page 37)* wherever you want. Doors, if required, can be attached to the stiles fixed on to the edges of the partitions.

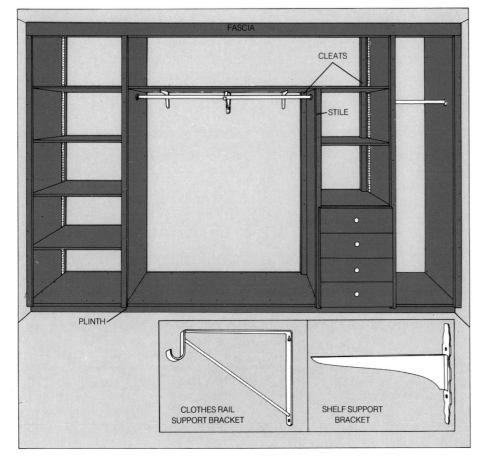

Three Designs for a Storage Wall

A wall-to-wall wardrobe. This room-width array of built-in shelves, drawers and clothes rails is divided neatly into vertical compartments by partitions that are held to the floor and wall by cleats. Bottoms for the compartments extend over a plinth, while a fascia borders the entire assembly at the ceiling. A short partition, convenient but just as easily omitted, helps support a long shelf and clothes rail that are elsewhere braced by full-height partitions and support brackets *(inset)* fastened to the back wall.

This combination of partitions, shelves, drawers and clothes rails is only an example—the compartments can be of any width and number to accommodate anything from skis to suitcases. Doors can be attached to partition stiles to cover all or some of the compartments.

A built-in round the bed. This simple adaptation of a storage wall incorporates a bed as its central feature. The partitions on either side of the bed are held in place by the same basic frame as that of the wardrobe *(page 61)*. The plinth and bottom shelf are omitted in the central compartment to allow the bed to fit snugly inside, and in the right-hand compartment to create a dressing table. To hide the floor cleats that would normally be concealed by the plinth, the frame stiles have been extended to the floor. A bedside shelf, supported by a pair of brackets, has been fitted to each partition on either side of the bed.

A storage wall for the living room. This wall unit is based on the same frame and partitions as the previous two units *(above and page 61)*. Here, however, the central area is used for extra shelving and storage. Two doors have been added at the bottom to make a cupboard, and above the cupboard is a drinks cabinet with a cantilevered door held open by stay supports *(page 41)*. Because of the weight of such items as a television, video recorder, drinks and books, the shelf span does not exceed 600 mm; if the span were any greater, there would be a danger of sagging.

Erecting a Storage Wall

1 **Dividing and marking the space.** Divide the distance between the walls into vertical sections, mark the sections off at the top and bottom of the back wall and snap chalk lines between the marks. Use the longer leg of a steel square to extend each vertical line along the floor.

2 **Installing partition cleats.** For all but the two side-wall partitions nail or screw 50 by 25 mm cleats to the floor and wall. Make wall cleats the height of the partitions, floor cleats 95 mm shorter than the partition depth. Locate the cleats 12 mm from the partition lines. If a wall cleat does not fall over a stud in a stud wall, fasten it to the wall with toggle bolts *(page 50, Step 2)* at 300 mm intervals.

3 **Installing the partitions.** After scribing the partitions against the end wall *(page 48)*, get a helper to hold each interior partition in place while you nail or screw it to the wall cleats and floor cleats at 150 mm intervals; at wall cleats that are fastened with toggle bolts, use 150 mm No. 8 screws rather than nails. Make the partitions, including two for the side walls, 25 mm shorter than the height of the room, and with a notch 95 mm deep and 100 mm long at the bottom front corner.

If the corners of the room are square, set each side-wall partition directly against the wall and nail through it into the studs; use plugs and screws in masonry walls. If the corners are not square, tack shims to the partition at the top and bottom and at 600 mm intervals to compensate for the deviation, and secure the partitions in place through the shims and into the wall.

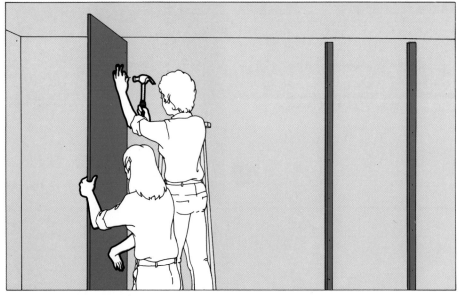

4 **Installing the bottom cleats.** Nail 50 by 25 mm cleats, cut to fit the sides and back of each section, to the partitions and to the studs of the back wall; the tops of the cleats should be flush with the tops of the partition notches. If the back wall is masonry, use plugs and 50 mm No. 8 screws at 300 mm intervals to secure the cleats.

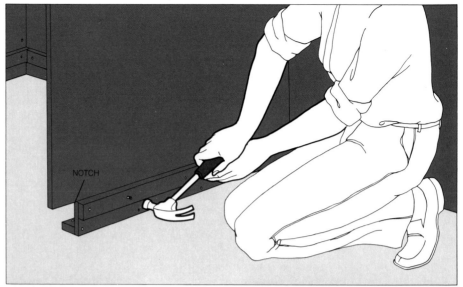

5 **Making the plinth.** Nail a board, 100 mm wide and cut to fit between the side walls, into the notches at the bottoms of the partitions. If you must use two pieces to span the distance, butt their inner ends at the edge of a partition; nail the end of one piece to the partition and the end of the other to a cleat *(inset)*.

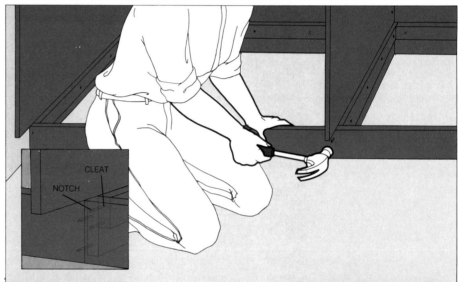

6 **Securing the bottom boards.** Nail bottom boards to the cleats at 200 mm intervals. Cut these boards to the full width and depth of each section and cut a notch in each board to fit it round a vertical wall cleat. Test fit bottom boards before nailing, and scribe if necessary so that they lie snugly against the wall.

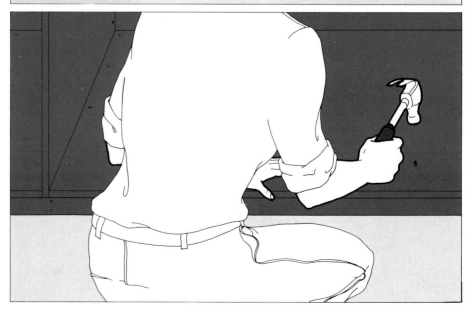

7 **Installing the fascia.** Nail a board, 100 mm wide and cut to fit between the side walls, to the top edges of the partitions. If you must use two pieces to span the distance, butt the ends at a partition edge and fasten a 50 by 25 mm block to one side of the partition as an additional nailing surface for the end of one fascia piece.

For a more decorative finish, cover the ceiling joint with coving *(page 51, Step 4)*.

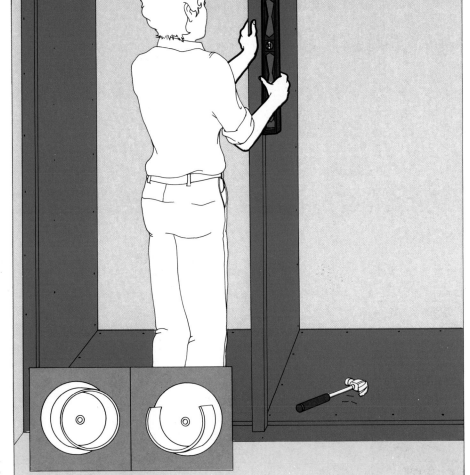

8 **Framing the partitions.** Apply glue to the front edge of each partition and, using a single nail, tack a 50 by 25 mm stile over its edge; check the stile for plumb with a spirit level, then nail it permanently in place at 250 mm intervals. On interior partitions, centre the stiles over the partition edges; on side-wall partitions, set the edge of a stile against the side wall.

Install shelves, drawers and doors by the methods shown in this chapter. Use end brackets *(inset)* to install clothes rails at partitions.

Furniture to Fit the House

A miniature sawmill for precision cuts. A table saw fitted with a dado headset *(page 24)* makes quick and accurate work of cutting stepped rebate and channelled housing and groove joints. The width of a cut depends upon the number of narrow inner blades, called spacers, that are sandwiched between two circular outer blades, called cutters; paper washers between spacers create fine width adjustments. When the entire assembly has been mounted, a wide-slotted plate *(right of blade)* screws on to the table round it.

There are several reasons for building-in furniture, some aesthetic and some purely economic. To an architect, the value of built-in benches, sofas, tables and even beds lies in the ease with which they can be integrated into the overall plan of the house, so that furnishings become one with the fundamental structures of walls, floors and ceilings, and the entire design is unified.

A plywood strip placed wall to wall across an alcove creates a bench that is more likely to appear to belong in the space than would movable chairs or a settee. It seems to fit because it does fit, you can construct a 4 metre bench almost as readily as a 1 metre one, suiting the scale of furniture to the scale of the room (and to the scale of the occupants, for you can adjust the dimensions of seats and tables to suit their users).

Built-in furniture looks like part of the house not only because it fits but because it *is* part of the house—a practical advantage on many counts. To a large extent a built-in is held together by the house structure, getting its strength and rigidity from the walls, floors and ceilings to which it is fastened. As a result, it is exceptionally sturdy; a built-in bunk-bed withstands juvenile bouncing better than most shop-bought bunks, and small children can clamber over screwed-down benches and tables without being tipped on to the floor.

The strength contributed by the house structure eliminates the need for the precise joinery of freestanding furniture. The techniques involved are those of the carpenter rather than the cabinet-maker. Thick, sturdy timber is used, and most pieces are nailed or screwed together (and to the house). Elaborate systems of springs are unnecessary; foam cushions or mattresses make plain wooden bench structures into comfortable sofas or beds. Similarly unnecessary—and generally undesirable—is ordinary upholstery; standard-sized cushions are readily fitted into home-made or shop-bought covers, and built-in sofas are often totally integrated into house design with coverings of carpet that run up from the floor and over them.

Because built-in furniture is simpler than freestanding pieces in so many ways, it is easy to build. It is also economical. A home-made sofa made of timber, plywood, chipboard or blockboard, screwed to the wall and covered with foam cushions and carpet *(pages 78–83)*, may cost only a fifth or even a tenth as much as a standard living-room piece.

This economy and simplicity frequently make built-in furniture the ideal choice for the less formal areas of a home: benches and tables for family dining, benches in halls, sofas in playrooms and holiday cottages, beds in children's rooms. But, appropriately designed, built-ins can adorn any room and fit into any decor.

Simple yet Versatile Seating: the Bench

A built-in bench, bed or sofa is easier to build than its freestanding counterpart, and a built-in bench is the easiest and most versatile of all. A shelf-like bench provides seating in an alcove. A box-like storage bench holds toys or linen without encroaching on floor space. More elaborate benches, with back rests and arms, can turn a kitchen corner into a breakfast area, complete with built-in table *(pages 90–93)*, or create a handy spot in a porch to sit while pulling off muddy boots.

All these benches can be assembled with simple housing and rebate joints, cut with a router or table saw, and strengthened by concealed glue blocks and hardware reinforcements. The easiest assembly is little more than a shelf fitted between the walls of an alcove—a plywood or blockboard seat, supported by three 100 by 50 mm ledgers fastened to the back and sides of the alcove, and by a fourth 100 by 50 across the front.

Because of the weight it will bear, do not use chipboard for a bench seat.

This frame provides all the necessary support for a bench less than 1 metre in length. A longer bench must have interior framing *(Step 4, opposite)* below the seat, and one or more legs: a single leg at the centre of the front support for a bench 1 to 2 metres long; two legs, spaced 1 metre apart, for a bench longer than 2 metres. Any of these benches—and any other bench you build—can be used for storage if you sheathe the front with plywood and hinge the seat *(page 73)*.

A bench fastened to a single wall calls for more elaborate framing. The storage bench on pages 70–73, for example, rests upon a ledger, a framework of 100 by 50s, and a set of three 100 by 50 mm plates anchored to the floor; the interior frame is covered on all its exposed sides by a skin of plywood, blockboard or chipboard.

A special problem in assembling a built-in bench is levelling the seat. In a bench built on site, you adjust the framing pieces as you go along. For an alcove bench, simply level the ledgers *(Step 1, below)*. Levelling a bench that is attached to one wall and partially supported by vertical framing is trickier. The heights of the vertical pieces must be set individually, either by using a level to determine their heights before cutting them *(page 70, Step 2)* or by scribing the cut supports *(page 77)*.

On a masonry wall, anchor the bench with plugged No. 10 screws or 75 mm masonry nails. On a stud wall use 75 mm No. 10 screws fixed into the studs; find the studs using the techniques on page 46 and mark their locations on the walls. Most benches are 400 to 500 mm high and 450 to 500 mm deep; if you plan to use the bench with a standard 750 mm table, make the seat 450 mm high.

Building an Alcove Bench

1 **Installing the ledgers.** Cut a 100 by 50 mm piece of timber to fit between the side walls of the alcove and make housings 45 mm wide, 9 mm deep and 900 mm apart for interior crosspieces. Level the back ledger on the back wall, 18 mm below seat height, and fasten the ledger to the studs of the wall, using 75 mm No. 10 screws; for a masonry wall, use 75 mm masonry nails.

For the side ledgers, cut two 100 by 50 mm pieces to the seat frame depth less 80 mm. Butt these ledgers against the back ledger along the side walls, level them, and attach them to the wall. Toenail them to the back ledger.

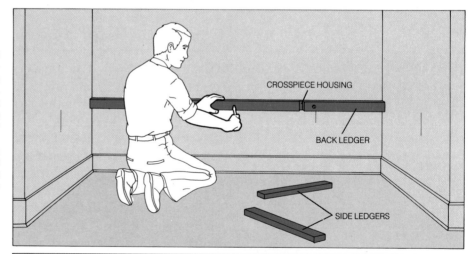

CROSSPIECE HOUSING

BACK LEDGER

SIDE LEDGERS

2 **The front support.** Glue and screw across the side ledgers a 100 by 50 mm piece of timber that is cut as long as the back ledger, has housings cut like it for crosspieces and has end rebates 45 mm wide and 9 mm deep. If legs are needed, cut housings for them in the front support; such leg housings should be 95 mm wide, 9 mm deep and no more than 1000 mm apart. Here, the front support has a housing for one leg at the centre.

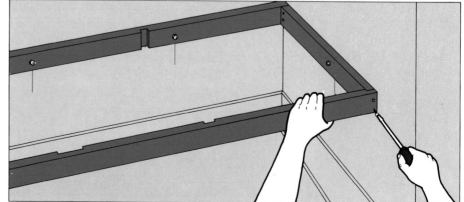

3 **Attaching legs.** If legs are needed, make each one from a 100 by 50, cut to fit between the top of the front support and the floor, and rebated at one end 95 mm wide and 18 mm deep. Fit the rebate into the leg housing in the front support and secure the rebated end with glue and screws. Toenail the bottom end to the floor.

4 **Adding crosspieces.** Cut 100 by 50s to fit between the housings in the back ledger and the housings in the front support. Glue the crosspieces into the housings, then toenail them to the back ledger and face-nail them to the front support.

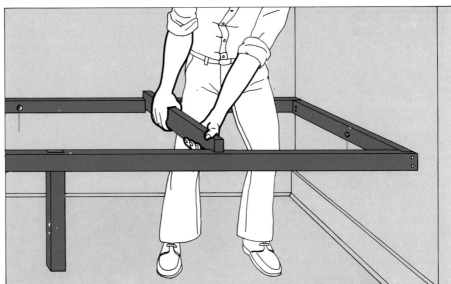

5 **Installing the seat.** Using the techniques described on page 53, scribe and cut a seat to fit the contours of the alcove and overhang the front support by 50 mm; glue the seat to the frame and, using a cardboard shield to protect the wall, fasten it with lost-head nails (*right*). Conceal the joint between the seat and the walls with strips of quadrant or scotia moulding (*page 47*). For an uncushioned seat, attach a 19 mm lipping (*page 29, Step 2*) to the front of the seat; if you plan to use cushions, use a 45 mm lipping, which will create a raised lip above the edge of the seat.

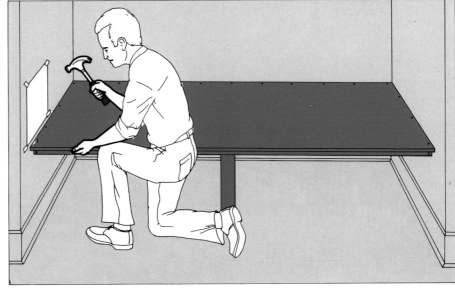

A Storage Bench with Interior Framing

1 Setting the plates. Cut two 100 by 50 mm pieces of timber, each 105 mm shorter than the seat depth. Cut a 100 by 50 mm piece that is 36 mm shorter than the bench length. Nail the plates to the floor, one end of each short plate at right angles to the wall and the other butting against an end of the long plate *(right)*.

For the back ledger and the front support, cut two 100 by 50s 90 mm shorter than the front plate. Cut 45 mm housings 300 mm from each end of these pieces, and fasten the back ledger to the wall *(page 68, Step 1)*.

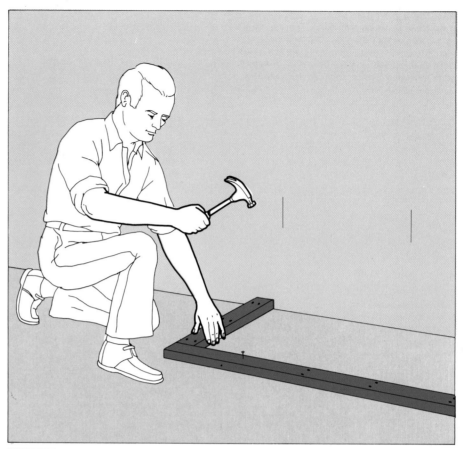

2 Measuring for the vertical supports. Set one end of a spirit level on top of each end of the ledger and measure the height of the level from the floor directly in front of the plate frame. Subtract 140 mm from each of the measurements and cut two sections of 100 by 50 mm timber to these lengths. Glue and toenail these supports on top of the plate at the two front corners.

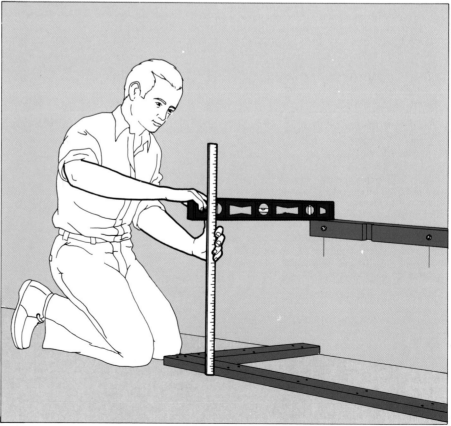

3 **Framing round corner cleats.** Using a cardboard shield to protect the wall, nail 100 by 50 mm side supports, 18 mm shorter than the bench depth, to the ends of the back ledger *(right)*, and glue them to the tops of the front vertical supports. Set 150 mm-long 50 by 50 mm cleats overlapping the joints between the side and vertical supports, use glue and nails to fasten them in place, then glue and nail the front support to the front edges of the corner cleats *(inset)*.

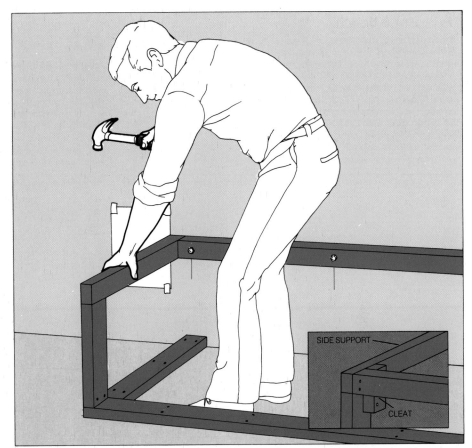

SIDE SUPPORT

CLEAT

4 **Installing the lid supports.** Cut two 100 by 50s to fit into the housings of the ledger and the front support, and cut a 45 mm housing 95 mm from an end of each piece; glue and nail the pieces into place so that their housings are at the back of the bench and facing each other. Glue and nail a third 100 by 50 into the housings of the lid supports. Reinforce the joints of all three pieces with cleats *(Step 3, above)* or with metal angle brackets, available at hardware shops.

Cover the sides and front of the bench with pieces of 18 mm board, scribing the back edges to the wall *(page 48)*.

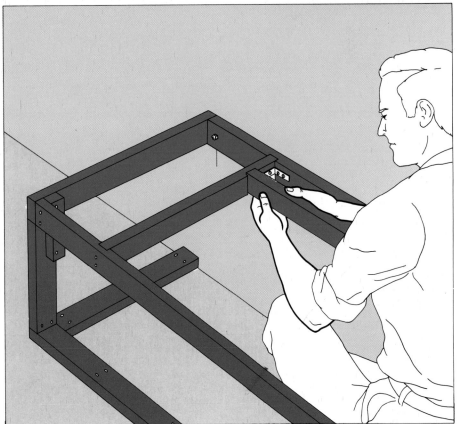

5 **Marking the seat.** Cut a seat of 18 mm plywood or blockboard to fit flush with the sides of the bench and to overhang the front by 25 mm; scribe and plane the back to fit against the wall *(page 48)*. At several points, measure the distances from the sides of the bench to the centre of the interior side supports and from the back of the bench to 25 mm beyond the interior back support; transfer the points to the seat and, using a trimming knife and steel square, connect them with lines for the back and sides of the lid.

6 **Cutting the sides of the lid.** Clamp the seat to a workbench with the line marking one side of the lid overhanging the edge of the bench and, using a straightedge guide and a circular saw, cut along the line from the front of the seat to a point 25 mm short of the corner of the lid, to allow space for a precise corner cutout. Complete the cut with a handsaw and repeat the procedure on the opposite side of the seat.

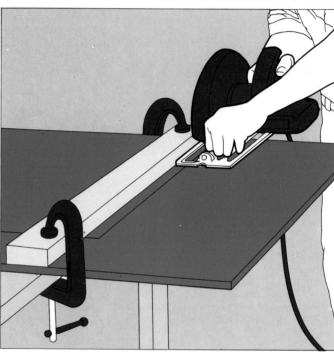

7 **Cutting the back of the lid.** Reposition the seat on the workbench so that the line marking the back edge of the lid overhangs the edge of the bench. Attach a guide beside the mark and set the saw with its base against the guide and its blade about 75 mm in from one end of the line. Push the blade guard forwards to expose the blade and tilt the saw on to the front edge of its base, lifting the blade clear of the wood. Turn the saw on and slowly lower the blade into the wood until the base rests flat. Hold the saw firmly—it will tend to bounce as it bites into the wood—and cut to a point 25 mm from the corner of the lid. Complete the cut at both ends of the line with a handsaw; the cutout will form the lid of the seat.

Use the saw to trim a strip from the back of the lid equal to 38 mm plus the width of the piano hinge you will use to hinge the lid. Sand the inside edges of the seat and the edges of the lid.

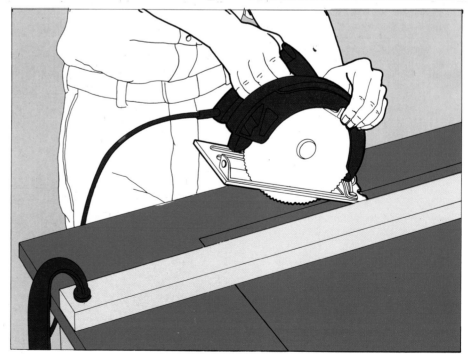

8 Attaching the seat. Attach the back of the seat to the top of the bench with glue and lost-head nails. Cut two strips of 19 mm timber, each 19 mm wide, to the length of the hinge line; using glue and 32 mm lost-head nails, attach the strips to the hinge edges of the seat and the lid. The strips *(inset)* will provide a fastening surface for the screws of the hinge, which would not hold fast in the edges of the board.

9 Hinging the lid. Select a piano hinge that has 18 mm leaves and, using a hacksaw, cut it to the length of the lid; fasten one leaf of the hinge to the wooden strip at the back of the lid. Set the lid upright at the back of its opening, centre it with 1.5 mm spacers wedged between its back corners and the seat, and get a helper to hold it completely open so that you can fasten the other leaf of the hinge to the strip on the seat.

To finish the bench, countersink and fill all exposed nail heads, and attach 19 mm lipping to the exposed edges of the seat and lid.

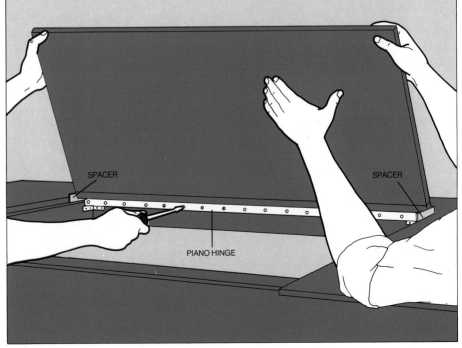

SPACER

SPACER

PIANO HINGE

A Bench with a Back and Arms

A bench built for heavy use—a bench in a dining area, for example—is more elaborate than one used for occasional seating. Its frame is similar to those on the preceding pages, but the installation of the frame is trickier, and arms and a back rest make the completed bench much more comfortable and inviting to sit on.

The example below is built as a freestanding unit, trimmed to fit the contours of its location, and then firmly anchored to the wall and floor. Using the same basic construction techniques, you can enhance the appearance of the bench by cutting its sides and back in curved or scrollwork shapes, using a high lipping to make a raised edge for seat cushions *(page 69, Step 5)*, or installing a sloped back *(page 80)*, if desired. For greater safety, round off any sharp corners with a sander or a rasp. Finish the rough edges with either iron-on or veneer tape edging. Alternatively, finish the straight edges with wooden lipping *(page 29, Step 2)*, if you prefer.

Like any other built-in, a kitchen bench must be fitted to its room, but some proportions are standard. The ideal depth for a seat with a back rest is 400 to 500 mm; the height of the seat should be 250 to 300 mm lower than the table it faces. Arm rests should rise between 200 and 250 mm above the seat; higher arms make access difficult between the bench and a table. A standard back rest is 330 to 450 mm high, although you may prefer a higher one to create a secluded dining area.

For the bench built with its back against the wall, follow the construction techniques described on these pages, with a few simple variations. First attach the back rest and a back ledger to the wall using 100 mm No. 12 screws; then, working out from the wall, add side pieces fitted to the contours of the floor.

Anatomy of the bench. The 100 by 50 mm framework of this bench consists of a front support and a back ledger, each with a housing at the centre for an interior support, screwed to two side ledgers. Two sides, shaped to form arms, rise from the floor; they are nailed to the side ledgers and screwed to the ends of the back ledger. Arm rest caps are shaped from short timber sections grooved to fit the freestanding side—made of plywood, blockboard or chipboard—and rebated to fit the side against the wall. A back rises from the bottom of the back ledger and fits into rebates cut in the two sides.

A plywood or blockboard seat, cantilevered 100 mm beyond the front support, rests on the frame and is glued to housings in the back and sides. One side of the bench is screwed to a wall; the other is fastened to a 50 by 50 mm cleat screwed to the floor.

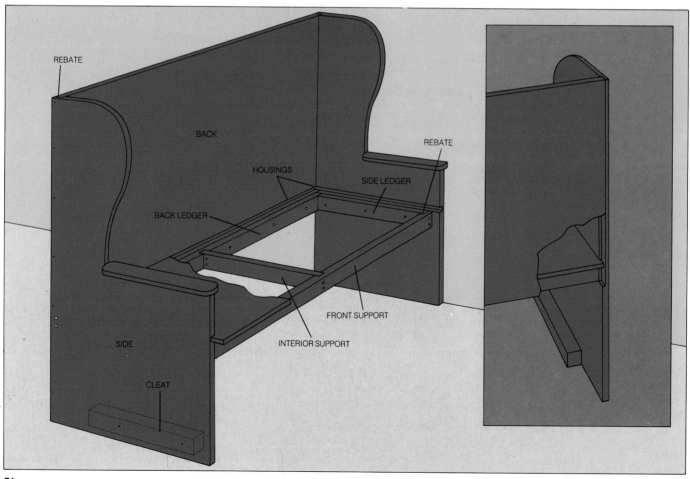

Building the Bench

1 Marking the pieces. Cut two side pieces of 18 mm board, shape the top and front edges with a jigsaw and, at the height of the seat, use a steel square and a trimming knife to mark the outlines of an 18 mm housing on each piece *(right)*. Directly below each housing, mark the position of a 100 by 50 mm side ledger, 63 mm in from the back edge and 90 mm in from the front. Finally, mark a line for an 18 mm rebate along the back of each piece, extending from the top corner to a point 95 mm below the bottom of the housing.

Cut a back with a height matching the side piece rebates and a length 18 mm shorter than the bench. Mark the back for an 18 mm housing 95 mm from the bottom, and mark the back ledger position 9 mm in from each end.

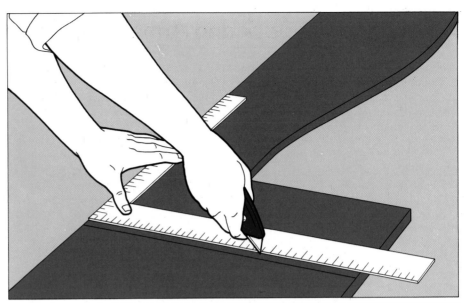

2 Cutting joints for the back. Use a router to cut rebates to a depth of 9 mm on the side pieces, then square the rounded ends of the rebates with a chisel. Set the bevel of the chisel blade facing the rebate and tap the handle gently with a mallet to make a shallow cut, then set the bevel upwards and drive the blade horizontally to shave out the bottom of the notch.

3 Making supports for the seat. Fasten ledgers to each side piece *(below, right)* and the back *(below)* by the following method. Cut 9 mm-deep housings in the side pieces and back between the lines marked in Step 1 and cut 100 by 50s to the ledger lengths marked on the sides and back; notch the centre of the back ledger with a housing 45 mm wide and 9 mm deep. Secure the ledgers with glue and 55 mm lost-head nails.

Using a 2 mm bit, drill two pilot holes through each side piece between the back of the side ledger and the rebate *(inset, below right)*.

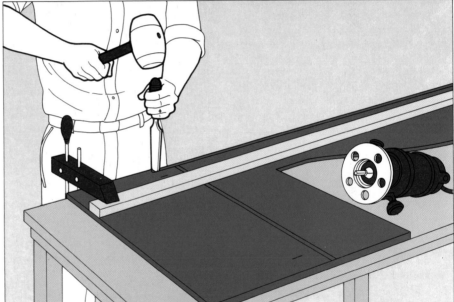

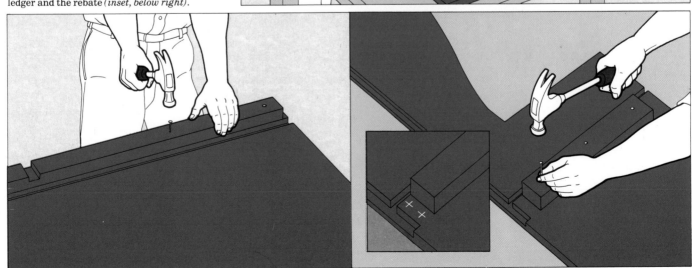

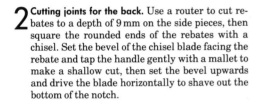

4 **Putting the pieces together.** Apply glue to the side piece rebates and to the vertical edges of the back; then, working with a helper, fit the three pieces together, using corner cramps to hold them square. Tack the sides to the back along the rebates, using lost-head nails at 150 mm intervals. Countersink two 67 mm No. 8 wood screws through the pilot holes in each side and into the ends of the back ledger.

Using the techniques shown on pages 68–69, Steps 2 and 4, complete the frame with a 100 by 50 mm front support and an interior support.

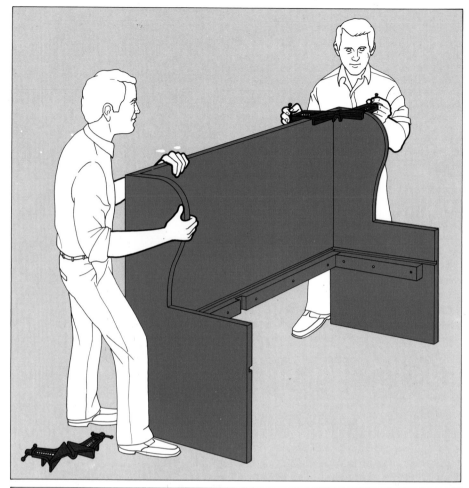

5 **Attaching the seat.** Cut an 18 mm seat to the length of the back groove and to the width of the side housings plus 50 mm; then apply glue to the housings and groove and to the back and side edges of the seat, and slide the seat into place. At 200 mm intervals countersink lost-head nails through the seat into the 100 by 50 mm framing beneath it. Glue and nail a 22 by 19 mm lipping to the front of the seat.

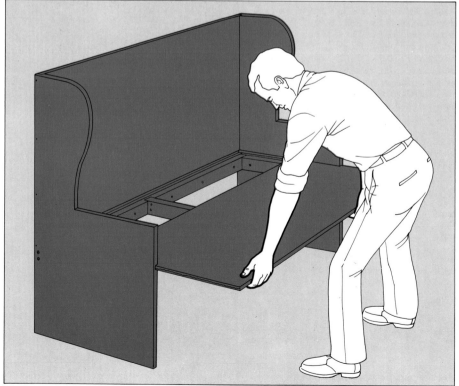

6 **Levelling the bench.** Set the end of the bench against the wall and, using a spirit level, shim the bench temporarily to level from side to side and from back to front. Scribe the bottoms of the side pieces to conform to the floor, then tip the bench over and use a smoothing or block plane to trim the edges to the scribe marks. Reposition the bench and check it for level.

Mark the position for a 50 by 50 mm cleat set well within the edges of the outer side piece *(page 74)*. Remove the bench and fasten the cleat to the floor with 63 mm No. 8 screws.

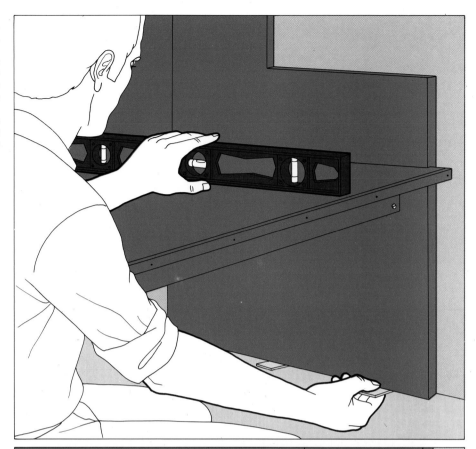

7 **Securing the bench.** For stud walls mark on the floor the location of the stud or studs behind the side of the bench, set the bench in place and use a combination square to extend the mark or marks vertically inside the bench and below the seat. Then mark points for screws to secure the bench—two points 150 mm apart for a single stud, or one point 250 mm above the floor in each of two studs. Drill pilot holes and fasten 63 mm No. 10 screws through the side piece and into the studs. On masonry walls, drill and plug two pilot holes 250 mm above the floor and 50 mm in from the side piece edges, and secure the bench with 63 mm No. 10 screws. Screw the other side piece to the floor cleat with 37 mm No. 8 screws at 150 mm intervals.

Make one arm rest from a 75 by 25. Round its corners with a rasp or jigsaw and, on its bottom, cut a groove stopped and squared 18 mm short of one end *(Step 2)*. Shape the other arm rest from a 50 by 25 with one flat edge to fit against the wall and a stopped rebate to fit the side of the bench. Attach the arm rests to the side pieces with glue and 37 mm lost-head nails.

Sofas Made to Order and Assembled on the Spot

More than its utilitarian cousin the bench, a built-in sofa meets the needs of interior design for odd spaces. A living room may have an alcove too small or a wall too long for any shop-bought sofa; a playroom or bedroom may have a corner for an inexpensive sofa that fills the space precisely. In many homes the answer to problems such as these is a custom-made sofa frame, blended into the room and fitted with cushions on the seat and back.

The construction techniques described on these pages can be adapted to make a variety of sofas. The furniture may be built between walls, or it can be flanked by end tables. The seat can be tilted 10 degrees for comfort; two tilted seats can meet at a corner table. If the seat is made level, two can join at a corner without an end table; three level-seated sofas can form a U-shaped unit. For a sofa back, the house walls can support wedge-shaped cushions, 100 mm

thick at the top and 200 mm at the bottom; most people, however, prefer a tilted back and straight cushions *(page 81)*.

In all these variations, the other sofa parts are fastened to the seat, which is supported in turn by the wall and floor *(below)*. Remove the skirting board and fit the sides of an end table against the wall or scribe the sides of the table to fit round the skirting board *(page 48)*. For a sofa built at right angles to a wall, support the seat with 18 mm boards fastened to the floor with 50 by 25 mm cleats, and cover the back of the sofa and end tables with manufactured board. The edges of these tables and of the sofa seat will be marked by long lines of rough board, which must be covered with tape or wooden lipping *(page 29, Step 2)* before the sofa is finished.

The length of the sofa will vary according to the location of the built-in: 2 metres will accommodate three people quite

comfortably. The depth from the front of the seat to the front of the back cushion should be about 480 mm, and the back height should be 400 to 600 mm if you want the shoulders supported.

Polyurethane foam in thicknesses of 100 to 150 mm is the material most often used for cushions. It is rated by density and hardness. Buy foam with a density of at least 26 to 30 kilograms per cubic metre—the denser foam is, the longer it lasts. Foam hardness, which can vary greatly between pieces of the same density, determines how comfortable the foam will be. On the solid seat of a built-in sofa, a medium to hard foam is preferable—one that will compress to half its thickness when the average person sits on it. For protection against fire, use a foam with a flame retardant additive and cover it with a natural covering such as wool, leather or flame retardant-treated cotton.

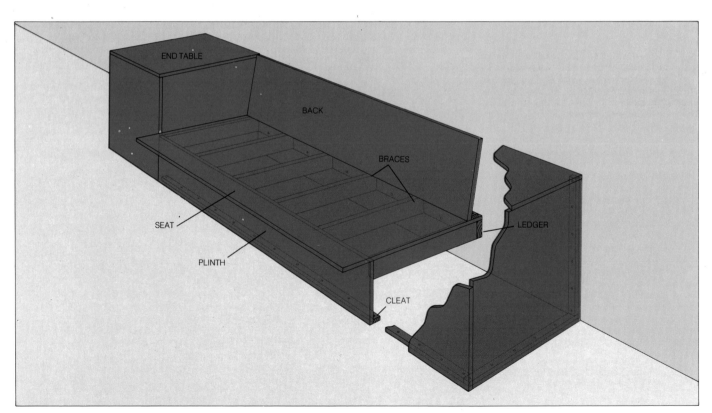

Anatomy of a built-in sofa. The sizes of the seat, back and end tables of this sofa can be modified to fit almost any space. A 300 by 19 mm plinth fastened to the floor, a set of 100 by 50 mm braces and a ledger attached to the wall support the seat, which in turn provides the base for an angled back. The end tables, which may be any height, conceal the ends of the frame; in other arrangements, end tables join sofa sections at a corner or along a wall.

Building a Seat

1 **Making the frame.** Cut a 300 by 19 mm plinth and a 100 by 50 mm ledger to the length of the seat; cut 100 by 50 mm braces 63 mm shorter than the depth of the seat frame. For a level seat, cut both ends of each brace square; for an angled seat, cut the ends parallel to one another but at an angle of about 2½ degrees to the face, following a cutting line *(inset)* marked with a protractor and sliding bevel. Butt-nail the braces to the back of the plinth at intervals of approximately 400 mm. Butt-nail the ledger to the other ends of the braces.

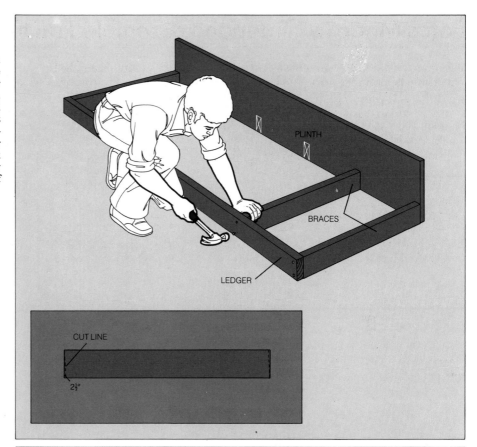

PLINTH

BRACES

LEDGER

CUT LINE

2½°

2 **Nailing the floor cleat.** Using a steel square, straightedge and tape measure, mark a line on the floor at the location of the rear edge of the plinth. Cut a 50 by 25 to the length of the sofa and nail or screw it to the floor, directly behind the line, at 150 mm intervals.

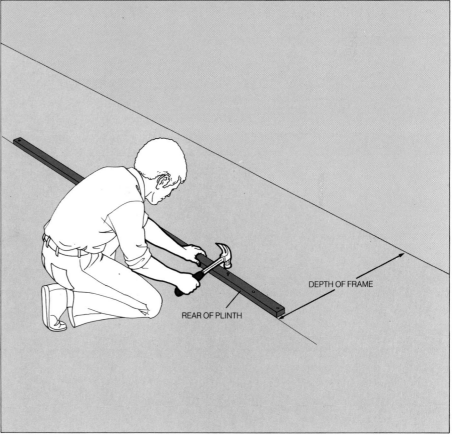

DEPTH OF FRAME

REAR OF PLINTH

3 **Fastening the frame in place.** Draw a line on the wall at the plinth height for a level seat, or 37 mm lower for an angled seat. With a helper, set the ledger in place with its top directly under the line. On a stud wall *(right)* use 87 mm lost-head nails to fasten the ledger to each wall stud. On a masonry wall, drill and plug pilot holes at 300 mm intervals, and secure the ledger with 87 mm No. 10 screws. Then nail the bottom of the plinth to the floor cleat at 150 mm intervals.

For the seat, cut a rectangle as long as the frame and 150 mm deeper; use lost-head nails to nail the seat to the ledger and to the braces at 300 mm intervals.

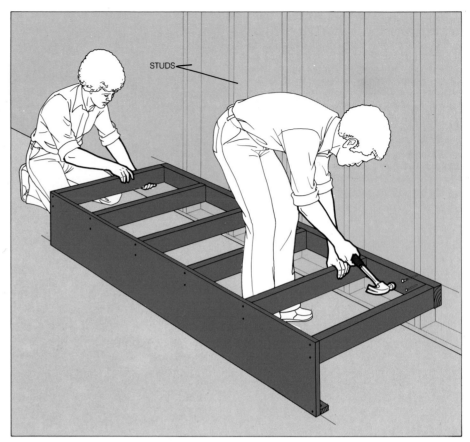

STUDS

Setting In a Back

1 **Positioning the back.** Cut an 18 mm back to the length of the seat and about 400 mm high, set it in place at the back of the seat and slide its bottom forwards until its angle matches that of a sliding bevel set at 100 degrees. Check the angle along the entire back, then use a pencil to trace the bottom edge of the back on the seat.

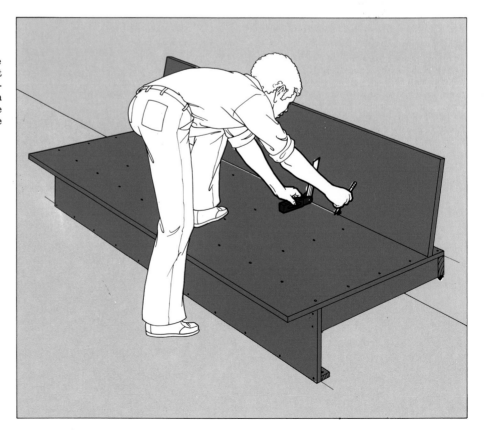

2 **Securing the back.** Slide a 50 by 25 mm cleat behind and against the back, and mark the cleat's position on the seat. Remove the back and fasten the cleat in place, driving 37 mm lost-head nails through the seat and into the braces. On a stud wall, secure the back by nailing 50 mm lost-head nails 15 mm below the top edge to each stud. On a masonry wall, drill and plug pilot holes at 200 mm intervals 15 mm down from the top of the back, and secure the back to the wall with 50 mm No. 8 screws. Finally, use 50 mm lost-head nails to secure the back to the cleat.

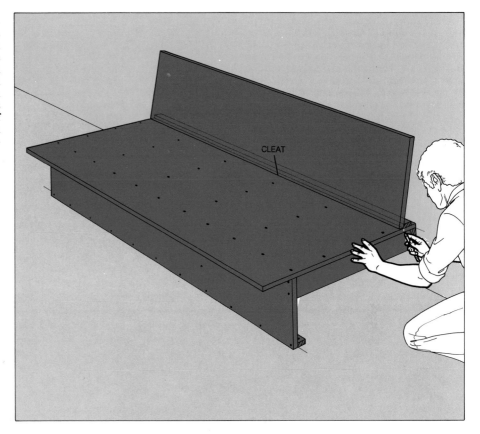

CLEAT

Adding an End Table

1 **The sofa side of the table.** Cut a rectangle to extend from the wall to the back of the plinth and to rise as high as the table, less 18 mm for the tabletop; nail this side of the table to the seat frame and to the back every 150 mm. If the height you have chosen sets the tabletop below the top of the back, cut and fasten a triangle to cover the back's open end.

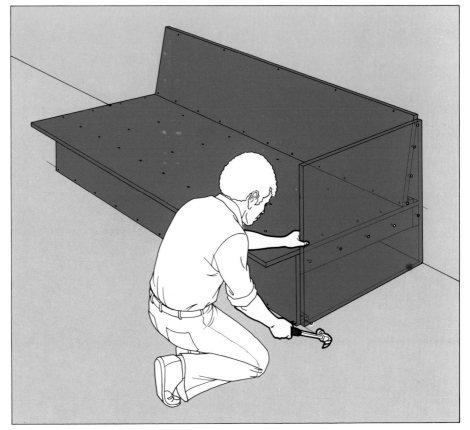

2 **Installing the cleats.** Using a tape measure and a level, draw two lines on the floor for the inside edges of the table front and outer side, and a third line on the wall for the vertical inside edge of this side. At 150 mm intervals, nail or screw 100 by 50 mm cleats directly inside the floor lines. If the wall mark is aligned with a stud, nail the third cleat to the stud using 63 mm nails; otherwise, fasten this cleat to the wall with toggle bolts. For a masonry wall use plugged 63 mm No. 8 screws.

3 **Completing the table.** Cut the outer side of the table to match the side that fits against the end of the sofa, and nail it to the floor cleat at 150 mm intervals. If the wall cleat at the back of the table area is nailed to a stud or to masonry, nail the side to that cleat also; if the wall cleat is toggle-bolted to the wall, fasten the side to the cleat with No. 10 screws. Cut and nail a front piece that will fit over the front edges of the sides. Cut and nail a top to fit over the sides and the front.

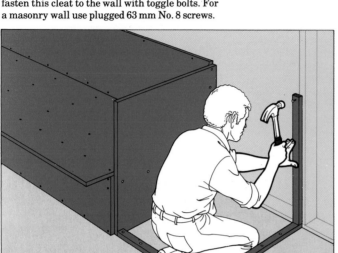

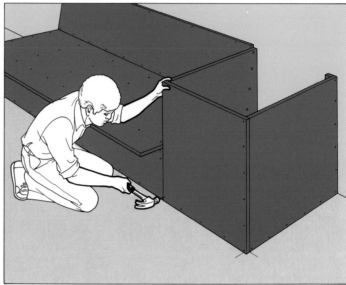

Connections at Corners

1 **Linking the frames.** Build a sofa with a level seat, butt one end into a corner and fasten the frame to the wall *(page 80, Step 3)*. Build a second, similar frame with an extra interior brace; the inner edge of this brace should lie 83 mm from the inner edge of the first brace. Install this frame with its end brace butted against the plinth of the first; fasten the second frame to the first, driving nails through the plinth of the first frame into the end brace of the second frame at 150 mm intervals.

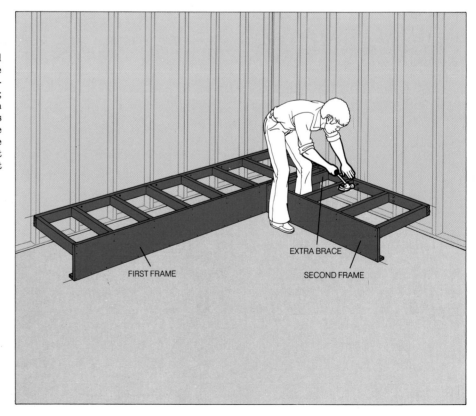

FIRST FRAME

EXTRA BRACE

SECOND FRAME

2 **Fitting the seats.** Install the seat of the first frame *(page 80, Step 3)* and nail the overlapping part of its overhang to the extra brace built into the second frame. For the second frame, cut a seat as deep as the seat of the first frame and wide enough to cover the exposed part of the second frame; nail this seat to the extra brace and to the other parts of the frame.

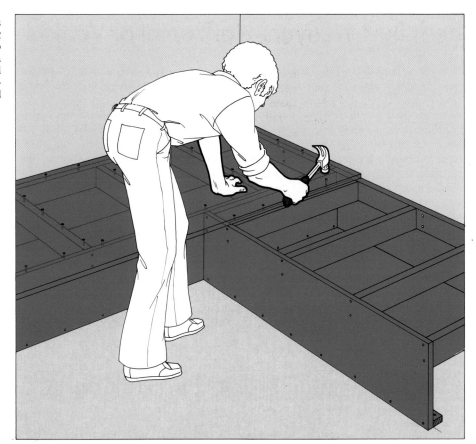

3 **Fitting the backs.** Install the back of the first frame to fit into the corner *(pages 80–81, Steps 1–2)*, then butt a sheet for the second back against the bottom of the first and, using a pair of compasses, scribe this sheet to fit against the first back. Cut the second back, at the scribed line, trim its other end flush with the outer end of the second frame, and nail or screw it in place to the wall and to a cleat.

At each open end of the frames, build an end table *(pages 81–82, Steps 1–3)*.

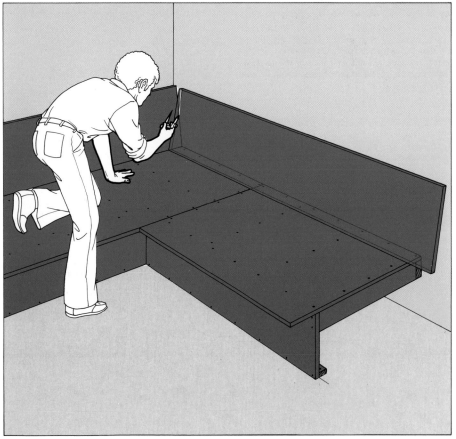

Beds Built in Layers, Horizontal or Vertical

In small or crowded rooms, freestanding beds squander valuable floor space and headroom—but the squandered space can be reclaimed or put to good use. A built-in bed that seems to vanish into a wall when not in use *(opposite page, above)* saves precious floor space; a pair of bunk-beds built in two tiers *(below)* makes clever use of wasted headroom. And an ordinary bed set into a built-in recess *(opposite page, below)* uses its headroom to good effect in another way—the curtained recess traps body heat and protects the bed from the draughts of a wintry bedroom.

The most dramatic space saver is the disappearing bed, which comes in sizes ranging from a small single (190 by 90 cm) to a standard double (200 by 150 cm). The frame of the bed swings up from the floor into a simple wooden cabinet; the manufacturer supplies the frame with the bed, but generally you must make the cabinet yourself *(page 89)*. The cabinet, which juts about 480 mm into the room, can be camouflaged with built-in shelving or cabinets on each side.

Two types of disappearing bed are available. The more elaborate and expensive has a panelled bottom that rises with the bed; the panel comes in a variety of finishes, or it can be finished to match the room round it. The simpler type of bed has an exposed metal frame that must be hidden by cabinet doors.

A built-in bunk-bed, like all built-ins, is fastened to the house structure. Because of this strong support, the frame can be made of 32 mm timber (which in its actual dimensions will be 28 mm thick), and will not require heavy corner posts. Although the beds can be built to hold sprung bases and mattresses, most people prefer to design them for shallower interior sprung mattresses, which leave room for drawers and shelves underneath. To increase headroom in rooms with low ceilings, use 150 mm sides rather than the 225 mm sides illustrated here. For a bunk-bed, use mattresses that are at least 100 to 125 mm thick and 190 cm long. Although 76 cm-wide mattresses are available, it is better to use ones 90 cm wide; small children, for whom the smaller mattresses would be suitable, soon outgrow them.

A bunk-bed. The floor, wall and ceiling provide solid support for this built-in bed; the bed itself can be assembled with thin boards and simple butt joints. Each of the posts at the corners consists of two butt-jointed 32 mm boards, one 25 mm wider than the other so that the sides of the posts are the same width. Three tiers of 225 by 25 mm sides are screwed into the posts and to 100 by 32 mm spacers at the wall; the two lower tiers are fitted with 50 by 25 mm ledgers and 18 mm boards to hold the mattresses. Nailing blocks at the bottoms and tops of the posts are used to anchor the frame to the floor and ceiling.

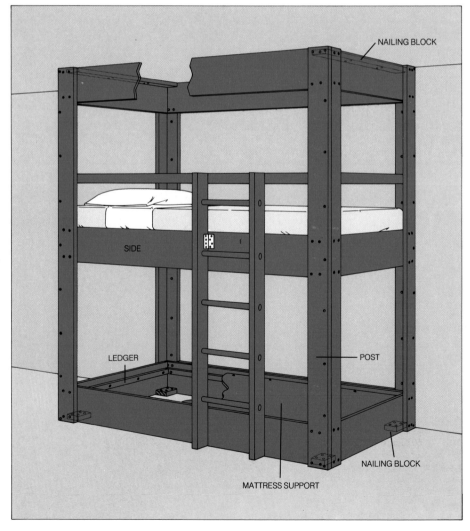

NAILING BLOCK

SIDE

LEDGER

POST

NAILING BLOCK

MATTRESS SUPPORT

A bed that becomes a wall. This disappearing bed is built on a section of wall framing covered with a panel. The frame is anchored to the floor with screws, driven through the bottom of a large cabinet. When the foot of the bed is lifted, spring-loaded hinges at the back of the frame help to draw the bed into the closed position *(inset)*, in which it is concealed behind the panel; handles on the panel are used to open the bed up again. The top of the frame is tapered to clear the top of the cabinet, and the mattress and sprung base are strapped to the frame.

A bed that disappears behind doors. This bed is anchored and hinged like the one on the left, but does not have a panel covering the bottom. Instead, the bottom consists of an exposed metal frame that is concealed by a pair of cabinet doors when the bed is closed; the legs of the bed retract automatically as the bed is raised. Because the bed bottom is not a wall of the cabinet, the bed does not need to fit snugly in its cabinet—it can be installed in a cabinet large enough to take bedside tables as well, or in an existing cupboard with a wide opening.

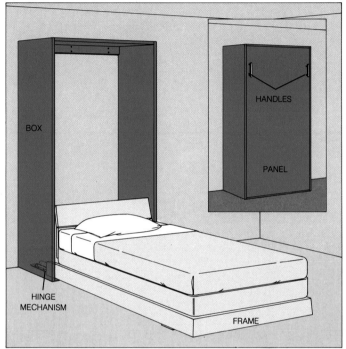

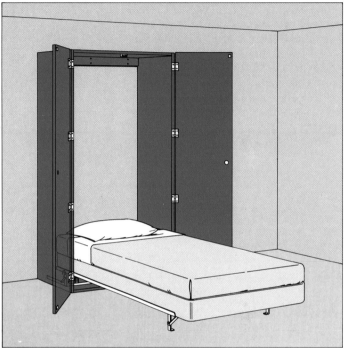

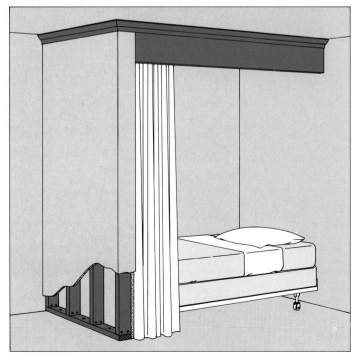

A bed in a built-in alcove. To create a recess for a bed in the corner of a room, a short wall is built of 100 by 50 mm studs and plates, covered with plasterboard. A curtain fitted with a pelmet conceals the bed by day and keeps off draughts at night; both the pelmet and the new wall are capped with lengths of coving to fit them to the ceiling. The metal bed frame rolls out of the recess on castors when the bed is made up.

A Sturdy Double-Decker

1 **Fastening posts to the wall.** At a corner of the bunk-bed location, countersink 75 mm No. 10 wood screws to fasten a 100 by 32 mm piece of timber cut to the height of the ceiling. Fasten to a wall stud, or to plugs if the wall is masonry, at 300 mm intervals; then glue the outer edge of the board and screw a similar 125 by 32 cut from 150 mm stock to it at a right angle, using 50 mm No. 10 screws. Install the other wall post 1900 mm away; on a stud wall, if there is no stud at the second location, use toggle bolts to fasten the 100 by 32 to the plasterboard.

Cut three 100 by 32 spacers to fit between the inner edges of the posts. Working at the stud locations, level and nail one spacer at the location you have chosen for the top of the lower bunk, generally about 225 mm above the floor; another at the top of the upper bunk, generally about 1300 mm above the floor; and the third at the wall-ceiling corner. On a masonry wall, drill and plug pilot holes at 300 mm intervals and fasten the spacers with 75 mm No. 10 screws.

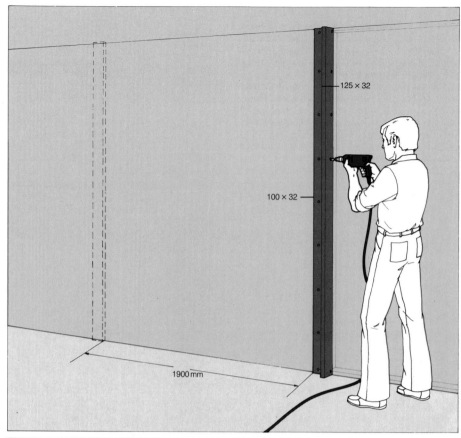

2 **Attaching sides to the wall.** Tack the top of a 225 by 25 mm board, cut to fit between the 125 by 32s in the wall posts, flush with the top of each spacer, and screw the board to the posts and the spacer with 75 mm No. 10 screws, countersinking four screws at each post and one at each stud (or at 300 mm intervals in masonry).

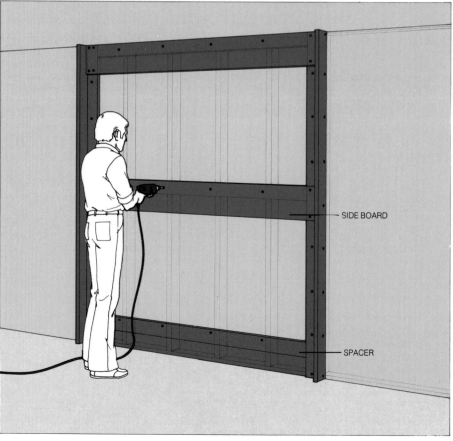

3 **Assembling and fastening the ends.** For an end assembly, cut three 225 by 25 mm boards as wide as the mattress plus 25 mm, then cut a 100 by 32 and a 125 by 32 the height of the ceiling at the other side of the bed location and screw the 100 by 32 to the three sides.

Tilt the end assembly into place and fasten its free ends at the inside corner of the wall post. Screw the 125 by 32 on to the front edge of the 100 by 32, then cut, fit together and install an assembly for the other end of the bed.

Cut a 225 by 25 mm board to the length of the wall side boards less 40 mm, and fasten it loosely to the middle of the front posts, using one screw at each post.

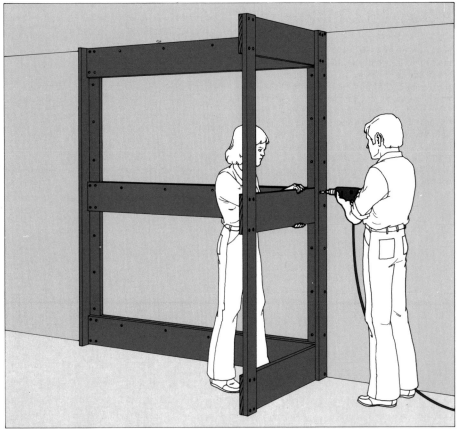

4 **Squaring the frame.** Measure the diagonals between the inside corners of the posts at the floor and ceiling. If the measurements differ, adjust the frame by shifting the bases of the front posts. When the frame is square and plumb, mark the floor and ceiling at the inside corners of the front posts and install all three side boards at the front posts. Be sure the posts are at their marks as you work through Step 5.

5 **Securing the posts to the floor.** Set a block of 100 by 50 about 100 mm long at the inside corner of each post, and nail it to the floor with four 100 mm round-wire nails. Nail the bottom of each front post to its block from both sides with 75 mm lost-head nails; nail the wall posts into their blocks from the open sides. For a wall post set into a corner, you need not use a nailing block; the fastenings at the corner are adequate.

6 **Securing the posts to the ceiling.** Fit 100 by 50 mm blocks running between the inside corners of the posts and at right angles to the joists above the ceiling *(right)*, and, using 75 mm nails, fasten the blocks to the joists. If the joists run parallel to the width of the bed, fit blocks down the sides, and fasten them to the joists where they cross. For a concrete ceiling, secure the blocks with 87 mm No. 10 screws at 300 mm intervals. Wherever possible, nail the outside face of each post to the end of a block.

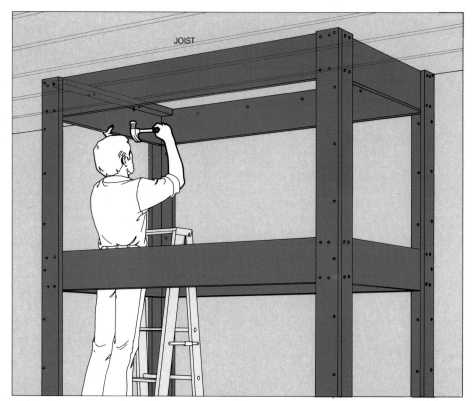

JOIST

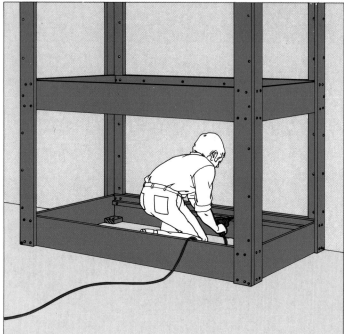

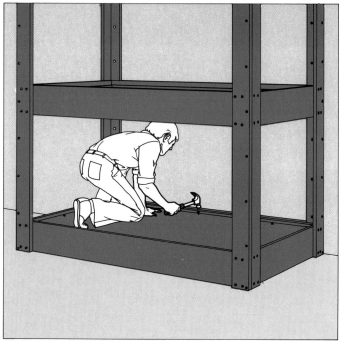

7 **Fastening ledgers.** At the bottom and middle tiers, glue then screw a 50 by 25 mm ledger to a side piece between two inside corners, setting the ledger 45 mm from the top of the side piece and using 37 mm No. 10 screws spaced at 300 mm intervals. Working round the tier, install three more ledgers in the same way, first fitting two ledgers between the end of one ledger and the next inside corner, then fitting the third between the ends of two ledgers. Leave the glue to set.

8 **Nailing on a mattress support.** For each bunk, nail an 18 mm blockboard or plywood board, cut to the inside dimensions of the sides, on to the ledgers, using 37 mm lost-head nails at 300 mm intervals. Mattresses can then be placed directly on these boards.

As guard rails for the open sides of the upper bunk, nail 75 by 25s between the insides of the posts 150 mm above the mattress. Make a ladder *(opposite page, above)* and install it towards one end of the bunk-beds.

A Simple Ladder

Assembling the parts. Cut two 100 by 38 mm stringers to the height of the front guard rail and drill 38 mm holes through their faces at equal intervals no more than 300 mm apart; cut 38 mm softwood dowels into 500 mm lengths, glue them into the holes with the end grain vertical and drive 50 mm lost-head nails through the backs of the stringers and into the dowels.

Either secure the ladder to the side board with right-angle framing connectors, or get a helper to hold the ladder up against the bunk-beds and secure two 76 mm No. 10 screws through the side board into each stringer. Then toenail each stringer to the floor.

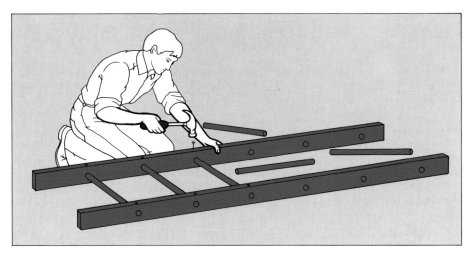

A Bed that Flips into a Wall

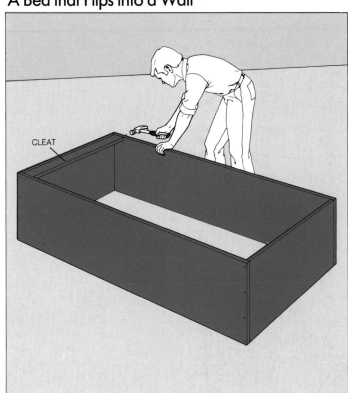

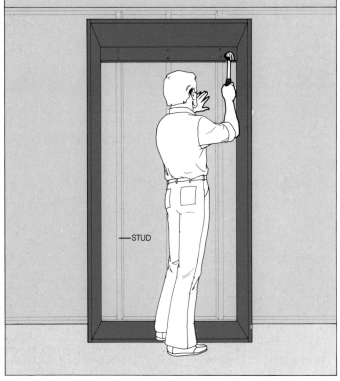

1 **Making the cabinet.** Build a four-sided 18 mm board cabinet, open on both sides. Butt-nail the sides to the top and bottom and fasten a 100 by 25 mm cleat between the sides at the top rear; drive the nails for the cleat through the sides and top. A cabinet made for a bed with a panelled bottom must fit the panel precisely, and the manufacturer will prescribe its dimensions; for a bed with a metal-frame bottom, the cabinet only needs to be larger than the frame. Tilt the cabinet up against the wall.

2 **Securing the cabinet.** Nail the cabinet to the wall through the cleat: for a stud wall *(right)*, use two 75 mm lost-head nails at each stud; for a masonry wall use plugs and 63 mm No. 10 screws spaced at 300 mm intervals. Nail the cabinet to the floor through the bottom using 50 mm lost-head nails at 300 mm intervals. Fasten the end of the bed to the cabinet according to the manufacturer's instructions. If the bed has a metal-frame bottom, add doors to the box *(page 37–41)*, preferably secured with magnetic catches *(page 41, bottom left)*. A bed with a panelled bottom needs no doors, but the panel should be finished to match or complement the walls of the room.

How to Build Tables that Hang from the Walls

A built-in table—or its higher, narrower cousin, the breakfast bar—is the most convenient furnishing for informal family meals. It can be designed to fill a space precisely—or to fill no space at all when not in use—and it is assembled, quickly and inexpensively, on the spot. It does not have to be in the kitchen, for it adds great convenience to a bedroom, playroom or breakfast area, and can convert a living-room corner into a dining area. A breakfast bar, generally 900 mm high, might be as long as a room; a table, generally 150 mm lower, can run as far along or out from the wall as its bench or pair of benches, and fit to any width between a bench and a wall or between two benches, so long as its edge is about even with the edge of the seats.

Stationary tabletops, fixed to a wall, are straightforward to build. One that fills an alcove can rest on wall cleats. When extended from a single wall, a table needs stronger support—a triangular bracket for a table extending up to 600 mm, one or more legs for longer tables.

A folding table or breakfast bar *(pages 92–93)* lies flat against a wall, so that it occupies no floor space when not needed. Use folding brackets, available in lengths ranging from 200 to 400 mm, to make such a

Three Designs for Stationary Tables

Cleats for an alcove table. L-shaped cleats, screwed to the studs, bricks or blocks behind the walls, support a tabletop set into an alcove, as shown here, or one set into a corner, with the free end of the table supported by a leg. The cleats are made of 50 by 25s; they are assembled with screws driven in at 300 mm intervals before being fastened to the wall. The tabletop is secured by screws driven up through the projecting pieces of the cleats.

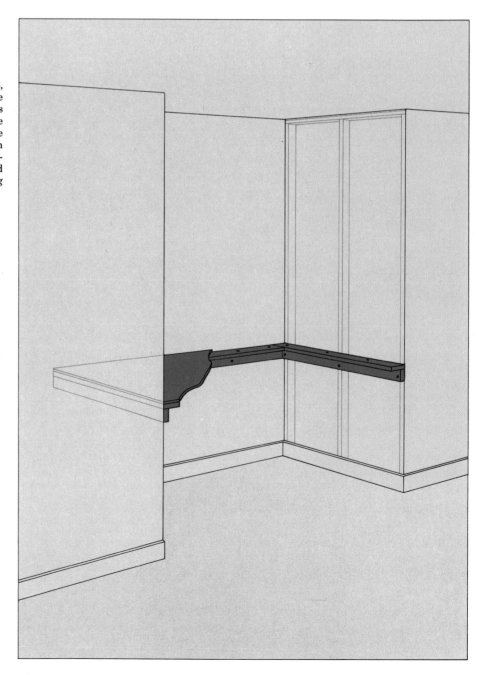

folding table or bar. Brackets can support surfaces up to twice their length; 200 mm brackets, for example, can be used to support a 400 mm-wide surface—an ideal width for a breakfast bar. The distance between brackets will depend on the use to which the folding table or bar will be put: a span of 1500 mm is sufficient for light use, but for a counter used by children who may lean and climb on it, not more than 1000 mm is recommended.

The tops for built-in tables and counters can be cut from manufactured board or timber, 12 to 18 mm thick. A plastic laminate surface may be preferable in some situations for its resistance to liquids and stains. For a large stationary table, a full-sized flush door up to 40 mm thick could be used. Legs for stationary tables are made of 100 by 50 mm timber for a cantilevered type, plywood or timber at least 12 mm thick for a panel leg.

Wall fixings can be safely and securely attached at any point along a masonry wall; for a stud wall, make sure fixings are sited at stud locations.

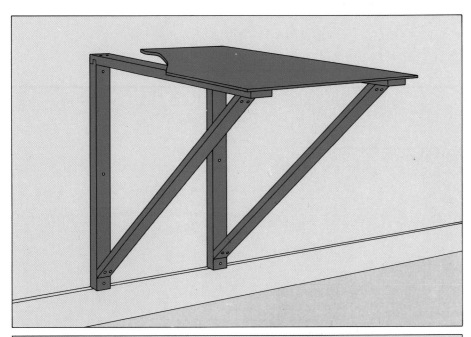

Brackets for a cantilevered table. A top extending as much as 600 mm out from a wall is supported by triangular 100 by 50 mm brackets. The vertical legs of the triangles rise from the skirting board and are screwed to the wall at top, bottom and centre. The horizontal legs, cut 45 mm shorter than the depth of the table, are housed to receive the ends of rebates on the vertical legs beneath them, and are fastened to these legs with glue and screws.

The diagonal legs, bevel-cut at top and bottom, are fastened to the other legs with screws driven through deeply countersunk pilot holes; the ends of the diagonal legs are set 25 mm in from the ends of the others, leaving room for a screw driven through the outer end of the horizontal leg into the tabletop, and for a screw driven through the bottom of the vertical leg into the wall.

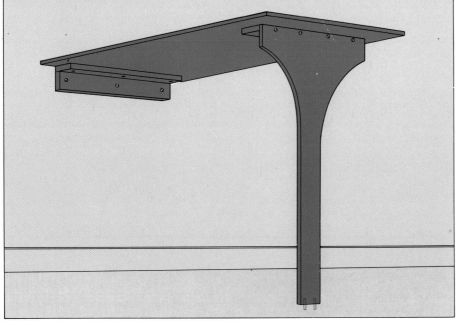

A panel leg for the end of a table. A top extending more than 600 mm out from a wall is supported at its inner end by an L-shaped cleat *(left)* and at its outer end by a plywood or timber panel leg, tapered so it will give firm support at the top and easy access under the table at the bottom. The leg is fastened to the floor with two dowels, 50 mm long, glued into holes in the floor and leg made with the aid of a dowelling jig *(page 33, below)*; its top is screwed to a 50 by 25 mm cleat, and the cleat is screwed to the tabletop.

Installing a Fold-Down Table Against a Masonry Wall

1 **Marking out the table height.** Using a tape measure, mark the height of the tabletop on the wall. Then, holding a spirit level at the mark, pencil a horizontal line along the wall the length of the proposed table.

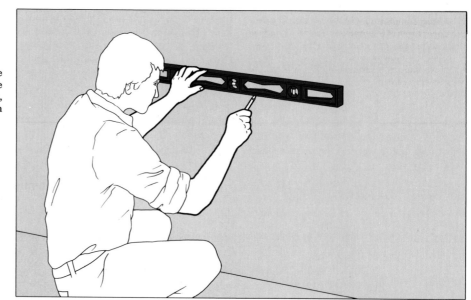

2 **Fixing the cleat.** To calculate the depth of the cleat, open out the bracket and measure from its corner to the edge of the hinge *(inset)*. Cut a cleat to this depth, the same thickness as the tabletop and the same length as the pencil line marked in Step 1, above. Ask a helper to hold the cleat against the wall, its top edge level with the pencil line, then drill through the cleat at 300 mm intervals to mark the wall. Remove the cleat, then drill and plug the holes; attach the cleat to the wall with screws *(right)*.

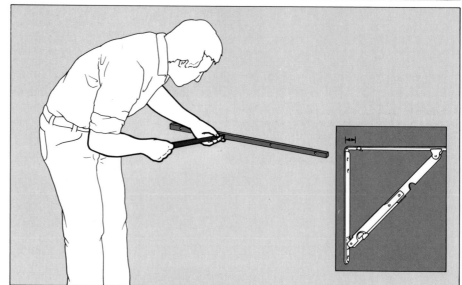

3 **Securing the brackets.** Below the cleat, mark two points 150 mm in from each end. Open a bracket and hold it up against the wall at one of the marks so that the top arm lies directly beneath the cleat. Mark the screwholes through the bracket on to the wall, drill and plug pilot holes and fix the bracket with 50 mm No. 8 screws. Fix the second bracket and any intervening brackets in the same way.

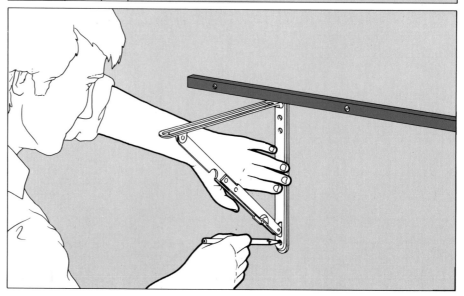

4 Positioning the tabletop. Centre the tabletop over the upper arms of the brackets. Insert a couple of 3 mm-wide spacers—small screws will do—between the tabletop and the cleat. This space will give enough clearance for the brackets to open and shut freely.

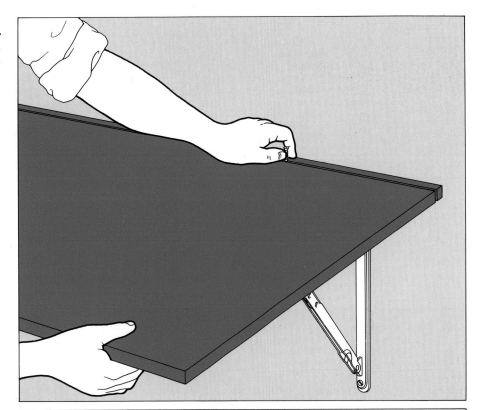

5 Attaching the tabletop. Get a helper to hold the tabletop down while you screw the upper arm of the brackets to the underside of the tabletop. Use a bradawl to start the screws. Before tightening the screws right up, remove the spacers.

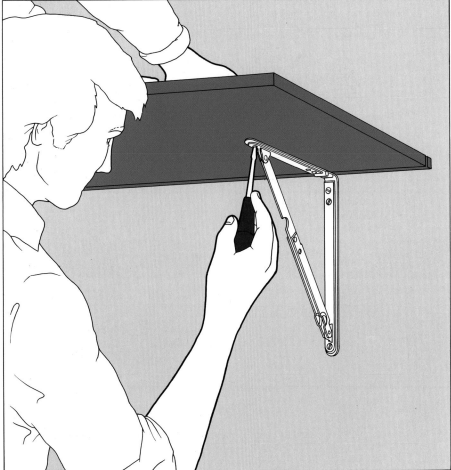

3 Special-Purpose Built-Ins

Special hinges for adjacent cabinets. A teak-veneered chipboard cabinet is fitted with an internal supporting frame *(top right of picture)* to make it a sturdy base for a built-in aquarium *(pages 108–111)*. To eliminate the need for a catch, the cabinet doors will each be attached with a pair of concealed spring hinges. The hinges are invisible from outside the cabinet and need no clearance when open, making them especially suitable for adjacent cabinets.

To fit them, the boss is inset in the door and the fixing plate is screwed to the side of the cabinet. The hole for the boss is cut with a special attachment fitted to a power drill.

In times past many houses abounded in rooms with special purposes, sometimes to satisfy an owner's whim, sometimes to help the household run smoothly. Even a relatively modest country house often boasted a billiard room, a library, a wine cellar and several drawing rooms.

Today's home owners have interests and needs no less special than those of their forebears, but the luxuries of space and scale are dramatically diminished. Even in a small house, however, it is not difficult to tailor a room to more than one purpose and to utilize space in such places as a basement or kitchen extension. All it usually takes is a few well-designed built-ins to accommodate a specific domestic or leisure activity. And what was prompted by a desire to put space to better use may also become an added attraction to a prospective buyer if you decide to sell your house.

A prime consideration for housing any activity is its special requirement for storage: a good rule of thumb is to plan for twice as much storage as you think you will need. Once you know the amount of storage you will need—and you have chosen a location for the units—you can design the built-ins. With a bit of ingenuity they can be fitted into corners or sections of rooms already used for other purposes. An area for washing and drying clothes can be turned into a finished laundry room with a worktop, clothes bins and a folding ironing board. Or a clothes cupboard can house a handy sewing centre—with a collapsible worktable, shelves, drawers and pegboard for storage.

You may also need space to accommodate other activities such as hobbies that have a tendency to overrun the house. The ideal solution is to find or make a space that can be permanently devoted to the hobby. But even when the pursuit requires a special environment you do not necessarily have to relinquish an entire room. The aquarium on pages 108–111, for example, is built into a floor-to-ceiling storage unit that will allow you to keep tropical fish without altering the function of the room. The aquarium becomes the focal point of the room, and the unit hides and stores such equipment as the pump and hoses. And the indoor garden *(pages 106–107)* that may have started as a single shelf of plants and rapidly expanded into a floor garden, is both a showcase and a home for prized species. By building a potting bench and storage units an entire room can be easily equipped for the serious gardener. In both cases—the indoor garden and the aquarium—the hobby and the room's primary use benefit from a doubling-up of form and function, with one purpose enhancing the other.

The Well-Equipped Laundry

A well-fitted laundry room can make the tasks of washing and drying, ironing and sorting clothes less onerous. It can be in a spare room, a kitchen extension or even in a well-ventilated basement.

In addition to such fittings as a washing machine and drier, the room should have an ironing board, a worktop for folding sheets and towels, and storage units to hold such space-consuming items as laundry baskets. The storage units shown on these pages are built from 18 mm-thick exterior-grade plywood and standard framing timber. They have butt joints, held together with wood glue and wood screws. Each completed unit should be sanded smooth, then given a coat of gloss paint to eliminate splinters that could snag fabrics and to protect the wood from moisture.

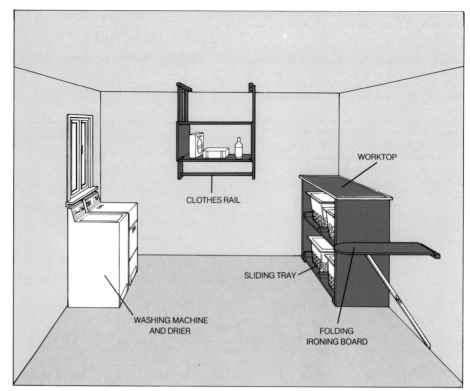

CLOTHES RAIL

WORKTOP

SLIDING TRAY

WASHING MACHINE AND DRIER

FOLDING IRONING BOARD

A well-equipped laundry area. In this laundry area arrangement, the washing machine and drier lie against one wall, while the built-in units are secured to adjacent and opposite walls. A worktop, useful for folding sheets and towels, tops a frame that supports two sliding trays, sized to hold four plastic laundry baskets. Suspended from the ceiling, a shelf unit with a clothes rail beneath it provides space for storing laundry supplies and for drying and airing clothing. The ironing board is situated close to the worktop and trays, and is secured to a wall cleat with a piano hinge that allows it to fold either up or down against the wall when not in use.

Building a Worktop with Laundry-Basket Trays

1 Installing cleats. To make a frame of 50 by 50 mm cleats, cut two floor cleats 25 mm shorter than the depth of the worktop, two vertical wall cleats 108 mm shorter than the height of the finished worktop and a horizontal wall cleat 86 mm shorter than the width of the finished unit.

Set the outside edges of the floor cleats the same distance apart as the length of the horizontal wall cleat, perpendicular to the wall, and nail them to the floor (use masonry nails for a concrete floor). Set the ends of the vertical wall cleats on top of the floor cleats, check they are plumb and fasten them to the wall. Then set the horizontal cleat across the tops of the vertical cleats, check for level and fasten it to the wall. For a stud wall, nail the cleats to studs wherever possible; otherwise use toggle bolts. For a masonry wall use plugged screws.

From 18 mm board cut two side panels the length of the floor cleat by the length of the vertical wall cleat plus 90 mm, and a top the length of the floor cleat plus 25 mm by the length of the horizontal cleat plus 86 mm. Glue and screw the pieces to the cleats and to each other; the top will overhang by 25 mm on three sides. Apply a finishing coat to the unit and add snap-on plastic moulding to the edges *(inset)*.

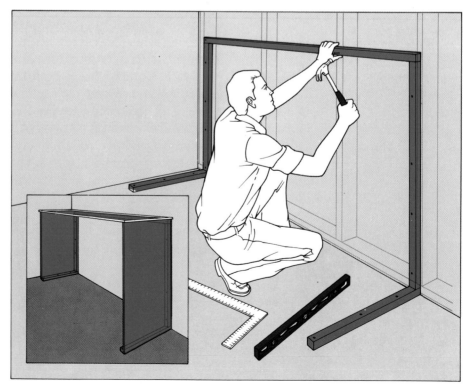

2 **Making the trays.** Cut an 18 mm thick tray bottom, making it the length of the horizontal cleat minus 25 mm by the length of the floor cleat minus 45 mm; frame the back and side edges with a rim of 100 by 25 mm strips, set on edge on the top surface of the tray bottom. Glue the strips on to the bottom, rounding off the front corners. Drive 38 mm No. 8 wood screws into the strips from the bottom *(right)*.

Cut a 50 by 50 mm centre support to fit between the front and back of the tray, fastening the support in place with 32 mm No. 8 wood screws driven through the back rim into the end of the support. Drive two additional screws through the tray bottom into the support, about 150 mm in from each end. Construct a second tray in the same way.

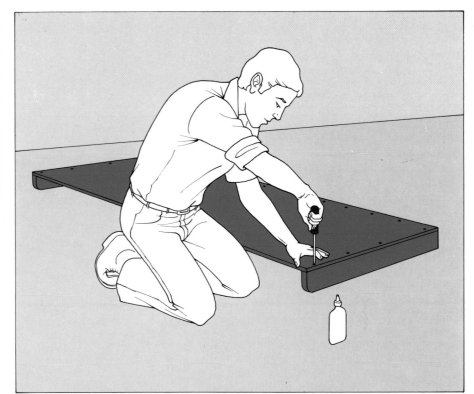

3 **Installing tray glides.** After marking level lines across the inside faces of both the side panels, one just above the floor cleat and the other about half way up, set the lower edge of a metal drawer-glide track flush with each line, and then mark the locations of the oblong screwholes. Drill pilot holes for these, and fasten the track in place with the screws provided by the manufacturer. Then screw the glides to the outsides of the tray rims at the positions specified in the manufacturer's instructions *(inset)*.

Slide each tray into place, and check that it fits squarely; adjust the clearances at the sides, and the depth of run if necessary *(page 36)*. When the trays fit, drill pilot holes for the circular screwholes, and drive in the remaining screws.

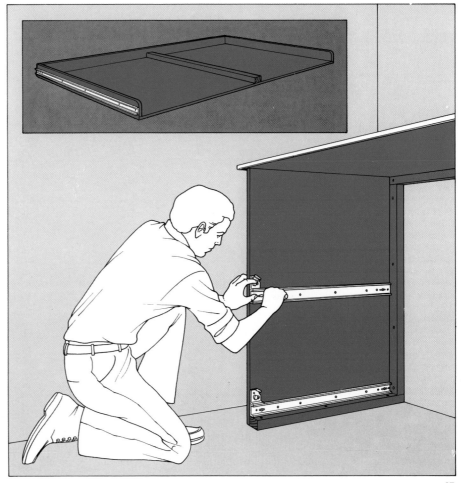

A Box of Storage Shelves with a Hanging Rail

1 **Installing hanging cleats.** To construct a shelf unit that will parallel concealed joists, mark parallel lines on the ceiling at each end of the proposed shelf span, long enough to cross two joists (at least 700 mm). Cut two cleats 500 mm long, and position the cleats just inside the lines so that their ends cross both joists. Fasten each cleat to the joists with two 75 mm coach screws.

To construct a unit at right angles to concealed joists, cut cleats 250 mm long, position them along the joists, and fasten them 50 mm in from each end with coach screws *(inset, near right)*.

For ceilings with exposed joists, cleats are not needed. If the unit will run parallel to the joists, nail a block between the two joists at each end of the unit span *(inset, far right)*. If the unit will run at right angles to the joists, fasten its side supports directly to the joist faces.

When fixing to concrete ceilings, drill and plug pilot holes at 300 mm intervals and secure the cleats with 87 mm No. 10 screws.

2 **Constructing the shelf unit.** Cut two 225 by 25s long enough to reach the outside edges of the nailing cleats, blocks or joists. Cut two more 225 by 25s, each 450 mm long. Glue and screw the four 225 by 25s together to form an open box with butt joints, the top and bottom of the box overlapping the sides. Reinforce the joints with eight 50 mm steel angle-brackets; position them 50 mm in from the front and back of the box, and fasten them with 19 mm wood screws.

Cut four 75 by 25 mm supports, making two of the supports long enough to reach from the ceiling to the proposed height of the bottom shelf, and the two remaining supports 300 mm longer than this measurement. Drill a 25 mm hole 100 mm from one end of each long support and round off the corners of that end.

Set the supports 35 mm in from the front and back of the box. Put the short supports at the back, lower ends flush with the bottom of the box; put the long supports at the front, holes extending below the box. Fasten each support to the box with three 37 mm No. 8 wood screws driven through the support and into the side of the box.

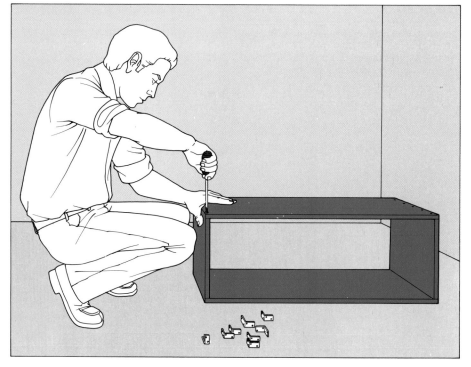

3 **Installing a clothes rail.** Cut a 25 mm dowel or chrome tubing long enough to reach to the outside faces of the front supports, slide the rod through the drilled holes, and secure it by driving screws through the supports and into the rod: use 32 mm No. 8 screws for dowel or self-tapping screws for chrome tubing.

Drill two pilot holes in the other end of each support, 25 mm in from the edges. Then, while a helper holds the unit in place, use 50 mm No. 8 screws to fasten the supports to the overhead cleats, nailing block or joist.

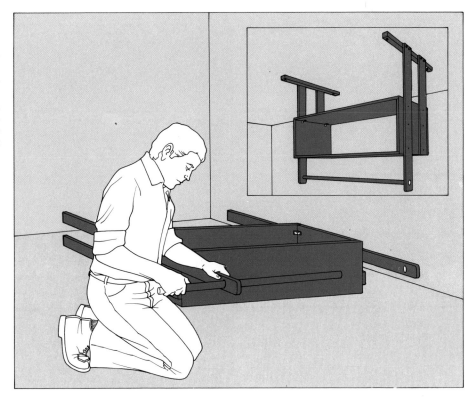

A Folding Ironing Board to Save Space

1 **Cutting the ironing board.** Position a standard ironing board, top down, on an 18 mm-thick piece of blockboard or plywood, so that the curved end is flush with one edge of the board beneath. Trace the outline of the ironing board and cut out the shape with a jigsaw. For a downward-folding ironing board, make certain that its length will be no more than its planned height so that it will clear the floor when folded against the wall.

2 **Hinging the board in place.** Cut a 50 by 50 mm cleat that is as long as the ironing board is wide, and fasten it to the wall so that the top edge is 18 mm lower than the planned height of the board, usually 800 to 1000 mm. Screw one leaf of a 19 mm piano hinge to the underside of the cut board at its straight end, hinge pin towards you and flush with the edge. Ask a helper to hold the board upright on top of the cleat while you screw the second hinge leaf to the cleat side.

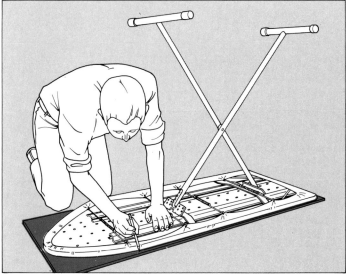

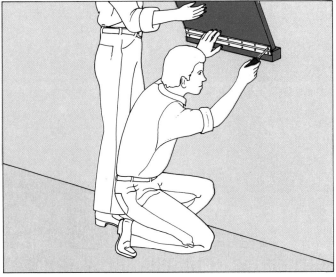

3 **Measuring for the leg.** Mark a spot on the under side of the board, 300 mm from the curved end and midway between the two sides. Get a helper to hold the board level while you measure the diagonal distance from this spot down to the bottom of the wall, directly beneath the midpoint of the cleat. Measure and mark off this distance on a strip of 50 by 50 timber.

Use a protractor and sliding bevel to draw a 48-degree angle at the mark you have just made, with the angle pointing towards the end of the 50 by 50 where you began the measurement *(top inset)*. Cut the mitre. When the board is open, the mitred end of the leg will fit against the wall where it meets the floor.

Cut the leg in half and fasten the halves together with a strap hinge, positioning the hinge on one side so that the leg will fold up against the bottom of the board. On the side of the leg opposite the hinge, install a bolt latch to keep the leg rigid when the board is in use *(bottom inset)*.

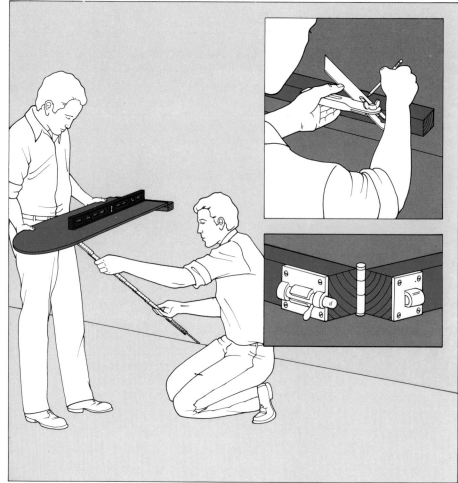

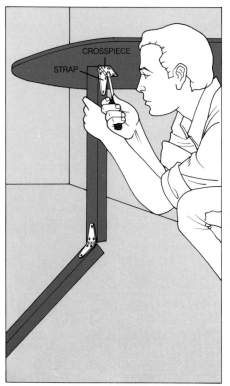

CROSSPIECE

STRAP

4 **Fastening the leg to the board.** Using a T-hinge, fasten the square end of the leg to the underside of the board at the point marked in Step 3, above. Screw the strap of the hinge to the end of the leg; then screw the crosspiece of the hinge to the underside of the board, lining up the hinge pin with the mark. Position the hinge strap in such a way that the leg will fold to lie flat against the board.

To keep the leg in its folded position when the board is stored flat, screw a hook to the underside of the board and an eye to the outside of the mitred end of the leg.

To keep an upward-folding board in place, fasten a second hook to the wall where the board tip meets it, and tack a loop of cord to the underside of the board, at the tip.

A Place for Sewing

Although the basic piece of equipment for a sewing area is a sewing machine, the range of activities that goes on there encompasses everything from cutting fabric to pressing the finished work. Thus it is necessary to find space for sizeable items such as a cutting table or ironing board, as well as systematic storage for the myriad sundries that are part of sewing—needles and pins, thread, buttons and patterns, fabrics and packets of accessories.

Ideally, a sewing centre should occupy an entire room, so that a project can be interrupted at any time without necessitating a clean-up operation. With some clever corner-cutting and careful planning, however, it is possible to create a well-equipped and efficient sewing area in a space as small as a little-used walk-in cupboard or wardrobe *(below)*. Of course, adequate light to work by, and at least two easily accessible electricity sockets are essential.

The sewing machine, if it is not already mounted in its own console, will require the support of a desk or a worktable. This should be 650 to 750 mm high, with a kneehole at least 450 mm wide and a top surface that is spacious enough to allow for easy manipulation of fabric as you move it through the machine. There should be minimum clearances of 300 mm between the needle and the back of the table, 600 mm to the left of the needle, and 150 mm to the right of the machine.

Storage space for sewing supplies should be as plentiful and as varied as possible. Even in the limited space of a sewing centre built into a walk-in cupboard, you will need shelves for see-through plastic boxes to contain fabrics and patterns, a roll-out chest with at least one shallow drawer for items such as buttons, thread and sewing-machine attachments, and a pegboard panel on the door for keeping scissors, tape measures and other sewing accessories within easy reach.

In more spacious quarters you could also hang a cork board on a nearby wall for pinning up instruction sheets for patterns, add open shelves or storage cabinets, build a folding ironing board *(pages 99–100)*, make a cutting table *(pages 90–93)*, and mount a full-length mirror to make hemming and fitting easier.

The most useful mirror is one with hinged wings that adjust to give you a three-way view. Such a mirror can be made from standard 1800 by 600 mm full-length panels, obtainable from glazing and mirror companies or department stores. These panels can be mounted with special U-shaped channels on a hinged plywood or blockboard frame, the centre section of which is attached to the wall. To avoid the possibility of distortion, use mirror that is 6 mm rather than 4 mm thick.

A Compact Sewing Centre

Converting a walk-in cupboard. This compact sewing centre combines a work surface, shelves and a chest of drawers that fit inside an average-sized cupboard when not in use. The fold-down table, 50 mm narrower than the door opening, is as long as the distance between the top and bottom shelves; it hooks against the top shelf when closed. Hinged to the bottom shelf, the table rests on a chest of drawers fitted with ball castors—metal-rimmed for a carpeted floor, rubber-trimmed for a wood or tile floor.

The chest of drawers can be ready-made or a home-made cabinet fitted with drawers *(pages 26–35)* in a size that clears the door opening by 50 mm and is 50 mm shorter than the distance from the door to the back wall. The combined height of the chest and its added castors should be 36 mm less than the desired height of the table. The shelves are 100 mm shallower than the depth of the cupboard, to allow clearance for the table in its upright position.

The sewing machine slides on to the bottom shelf when not in use. Do not attach it to the table; its weight would make the table difficult and dangerous to operate.

A Foldaway to Save Space

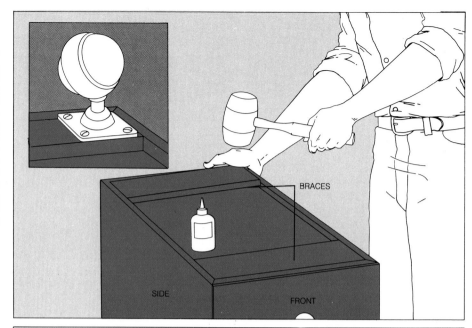

1 **Mounting castors on a chest.** To reinforce the bottom of a chest of drawers for mounting castors, glue and screw 75 by 25 mm braces to the front and the back. Drive the screws into the braces from the side of the chest, or remove the bottom drawer and drive screws through the chest bottom into the braces. If the bottom is recessed, as shown here, cut the braces to fit snugly between the sides, and tap them into position with a mallet; if the bottom is flush with the sides, surface-mount the braces. Use PVA glue and 38 mm woodscrews. When the glue is dry, place plate ball castors *(inset)* at each corner, and mark the positions of screwholes. Drill pilot holes, and attach the castors to the braces with the screws supplied with the castors.

2 **Installing the shelves.** Use a spirit level and a pencil to mark a horizontal line on one wall of the cupboard, 18 mm lower than the desired height of the bottom shelf and table. Cut a 50 by 25 mm cleat long enough to span the depth of the shelf and, after locating the studs in the wall *(page 46)* drive 63 mm nails through the cleat into each stud, positioning the top of the cleat flush with the marked line. In masonry, drill pilot holes and secure the cleat with plugged 63 mm No. 8 screws. Again using a level, mark lines at the same height on the back wall and the opposite wall. Attach a second cleat to the opposite wall. Then join the two cleats with a third, across the back wall. Install cleats for the other shelves in the same manner, making sure the second shelf will be high enough above the first to clear the sewing machine.

Cut shelves from 18 mm manufactured board and lay them on top of the cleats; for convenience in cleaning, do not fasten them in place.

3 **Making the table.** Measure and cut the fold-down tabletop from 18 mm manufactured board. The length should equal the distance from the bottom of the lowest shelf to the bottom of the top shelf; the width should be 50 mm narrower than the door. Then cut a 50 mm wide and 18 mm thick spacer board, 50 mm shorter than the table width, to lift the tabletop above the top of the supporting chest. Screw the spacer board to the underside of the table 150 mm from the outer end, centring it between the sides of the table. Glue a piece of felt or other soft material to the spacer board, to protect the chest top.

Cut a piece of 18 mm piano hinge to the table width. Screw it to the other end of the table, keeping the hinge pin flush with the tabletop.

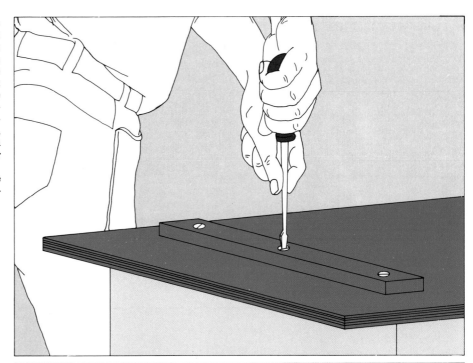

4 **Installing the table.** Get someone to hold the tabletop while you screw the other leaf of the piano hinge to the edge of the bottom shelf. Make sure that the surfaces of the table and shelf are flush when the table is folded down, and that the tabletop is centred in the door opening. Complete the installation by screwing a hook to the outer edge of the table and an eye to the corresponding point on the edge of the top shelf. Sand all edges well to avoid snags; fill in imperfections with wood filler; then finish with paint or polyurethane varnish *(pages 42–43)*.

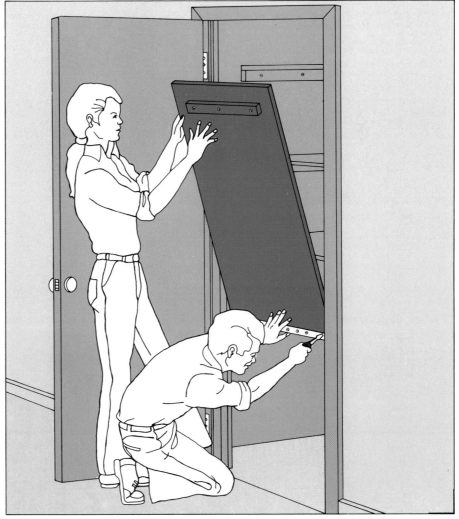

A Mirror that Opens for Viewing All Sides

1 Hinging the backing panels. Cut three backing panels from 18 mm blockboard or plywood, the same width as the mirror panels and 6 mm longer. Cut two pieces of 25 mm-wide piano hinge, the same length as the backing panels. Screw one leaf of each hinge to an edge of the centre panel, positioning each hinge so that its hinge pin is 6 mm above the panel's front face. Drill pilot holes first, then secure each hinge leaf with 19 mm No. 4 screws to ensure sufficient holding power. Screw the other leaf of each hinge to an edge of each side panel, hinge pins again 6 mm above the front of the panel.

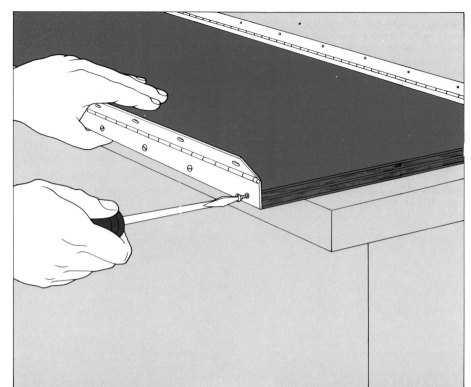

2 Attaching mirror channels. Using a hacksaw, cut lengths of U-shaped aluminium mirror channel to fit the top and bottom of each panel; use channel with a wide lip for the top, a narrow lip for the bottom. Secure the channel to the panels with 12 mm No. 4 screws at 50 mm intervals, placing the bottom of each channel flush with the edge of the panel. Cover the screw heads with masking tape to protect the mirrors.

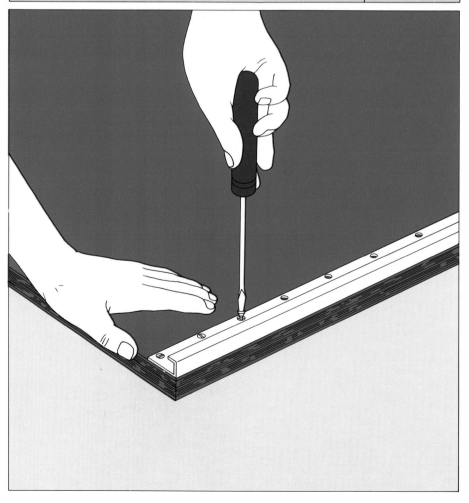

3 **Hanging the unit.** For a stud wall, locate the studs and ask a helper to hold the unit against the wall so that the centre panel spans two studs; drive two 50 mm nails through the panel into the studs, to hold it in place temporarily. Mark the stud locations on the face of the centre panel, and drill pilot holes at 300 mm intervals to accommodate 63 mm No. 8 wood screws. Drive the screws through the unit into the studs. Be sure to countersink all screws and nails slightly; then cover the heads with masking tape.

If you are hanging the mirror on a brick or block wall, drill and plug pilot holes 75 mm in from each corner, and down each side of the panel at 300 mm intervals, and secure the unit with 63 mm No. 8 screws.

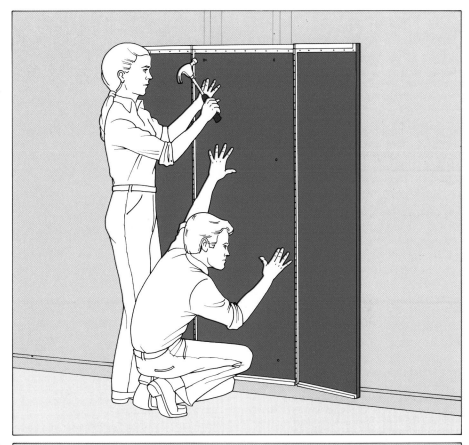

4 **Inserting the mirrors.** Pad the lower channel of the centre panel with 10 by 5 mm cushioning blocks, made from rubber or foam and placed 50 mm in from each end. With the aid of a helper, slide a mirror into the deep top channel, then gently lower it into the shallow bottom channel. Install mirrors in each of the two side wings in the same way. Finish the outside edge of each wing with a strip of 25 mm-wide wood or plastic edging, glued and fastened to the edge with panel pins. Finally, paint or varnish the edgings and the backs of the side wings.

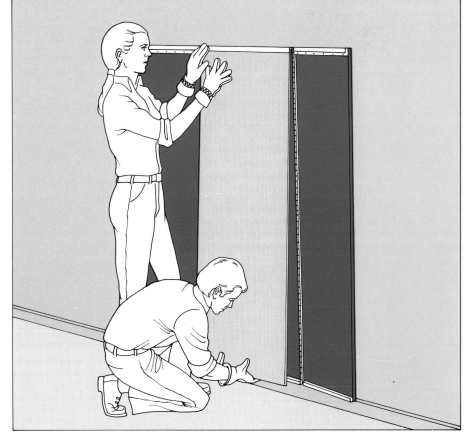

Creating an Indoor Garden

The floor garden shown here is an excellent showcase for plants. Situated near a light source, it can be used as a decorative feature in any room. Alternatively, it can be part of an indoor gardening area or gardening room fitted with a potting bench, nursery unit and storage for such gardening essentials as soil, fertilizers, chemicals for pest control, tools, pots, stakes and string, and a watering can.

Among possible locations for an indoor garden are an enclosed porch, a conservatory or a basement—areas where the existing flooring is more or less impervious to water damage. Ideally, the site should admit some natural light, preferably from south-facing windows (north-facing in the southern hemisphere). If natural light is limited it can be supplemented by or replaced with fluorescent light.

Fluorescent tubes produce an even light containing a high amount of blue rays—the rays that encourage luxuriant foliage. They also produce less heat and are less likely to scorch plants than ordinary incandescent bulbs. Mount the tubes in a reflector 450 to 600 mm above the plants and, for even more light, paint the garden and surrounding area in white gloss paint. Tubes may be mounted singly or in pairs: a pair of 1200 mm-long 40 watt tubes will illuminate an area 1200 by 300 mm; a 2400 mm-long 85 watt tube will illuminate a 2400 by 150 mm area.

For durability, the floor garden and any other structures in the gardening room should be made of Douglas fir, cedar, a wood that has been pressure-treated with a wood preservative harmless to plants, or exterior-grade plywood, and they should be put together with sherardized nails. For convenient watering, none of the planting units should be deeper than arm's length—usually about 600 mm.

A base for an indoor garden. This simple floor garden has a tray-like aluminium bottom that rests on slats inside a shallow wooden frame, which in turn is fixed to the wall. The frame sides may be constructed from either 150 by 25 mm timber treated with a wood preservative harmless to plants, or exterior-grade plywood, and should be assembled using sherardized nails which will not rust.

Boxing in a Floor Garden

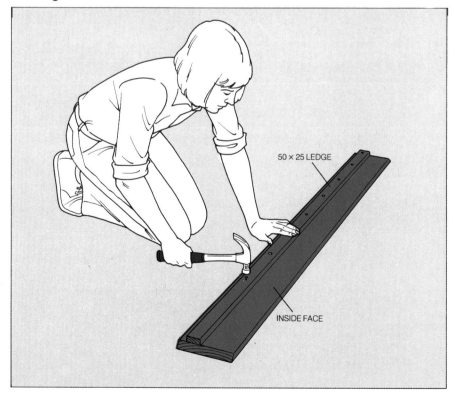

50 × 25 LEDGE

INSIDE FACE

1 **Attaching supports for slats.** Measure and cut four pieces of 150 by 25 mm timber or 150 by 18 mm exterior grade plywood for the box sides, mitring their ends at a 45-degree angle; plan the inside dimensions of the box to enclose the aluminium liner. Nail a supporting ledge of 50 by 25 mm timber to the inside face of each of the two long parallel sides of the box, positioning each ledge 10 mm above the lower edge of the box and flush with the ends of the side *(above)*. Use 37 mm sherardized nails, spaced 150 mm apart, to secure the ledges.

2 **Assembling the box.** Place two adjoining sides in a corner cramp, and check the joint for fit. If the mitred ends do not fit snugly, remove the sides from the clamp and lightly plane the high spots. Repeat the clamping and planing procedure until the two ends fit exactly. Apply a waterproof glue to both surfaces of the joint, and clamp until dry. Before removing the cramp, drive two lost-head nails into the joint from each side; set them with a nail punch. Repeat for the remaining joints. Fill the holes with wood filler.

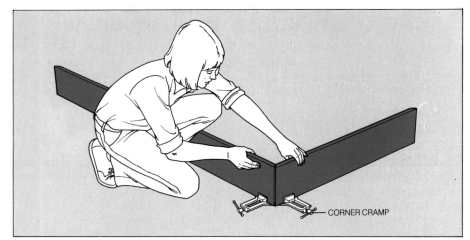

CORNER CRAMP

3 **Finishing the bottom.** Cut 50 by 25 mm slats to fit on edge between the ledges; space the slats about 200 mm apart. Nail a slat across the two ledges at each end of the box, using 63 mm lost-head nails and butting each end slat against the short sides of the box. Add the remaining slats. Screw or nail one long side to the wall or skirting board at 300 mm intervals.

4 **Making an aluminium liner.** From a builders' merchant or sheet-metal supplier, obtain a sheet of 24 gauge (0.56 mm) aluminium, 100 mm wider and longer than the inside of the box. Place the sheet on a work surface at least 100 mm shorter and narrower than the sheet, and allow one edge of the sheet to overhang by 50 mm. Put a weight on the sheet and then, wearing protective gloves, bend down the overhanging edge, pounding the crease smooth with a rubber mallet. Slide the sheet until a second, adjoining edge overhangs the work surface by 50 mm and, with tin snips, cut along the crease for 50 mm, forming a 50 mm square tab. Snip about 25 mm off the end, and taper the two vertical edges of the tab; then bend and smooth the second edge of the sheet, and tuck the tab under the first edge. Crease the sheet, cutting and forming tabs to shape the edges. Caulk the tabs with silicone sealant *(inset)*. Set the liner in the box. Place potted plants in the liner, over a 15 mm-deep layer of gravel, sand or marble chips.

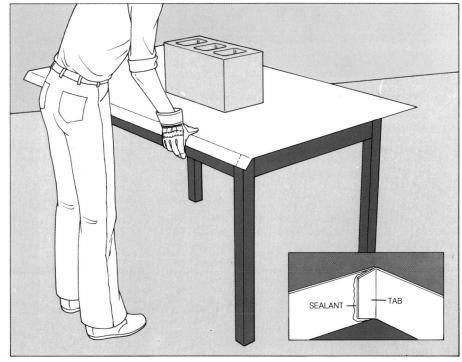

SEALANT — TAB

Building a Spectacular Wall Aquarium

A frieze of built-in aquariums can turn a blank wall into a showcase, or it can divide a large room with a wall of live entertainment visible from both sides. Whether your built-in holds a single aquarium tank or a series of them, the project requires consideration for both your fish and your house. The tremendous weight of water in a tank necessitates strong support, and the filtration system must be unobtrusive but easily accessible.

In setting up a large aquarium, location is important. You must place the tank or tanks well away from sunlit windows, because algae thrive in light, and will quickly clog up tanks. It is also best to keep tanks away from radiators and draughts, since most kinds of fish cannot endure rapid changes of temperature.

Space, however, is usually not a problem, because even the largest aquarium tanks are compact. A typical tank—600 mm long, 400 mm high and 300 mm wide—holds 58 litres; a tank the same height and width but 1200 mm long holds 116 litres. If you have room for a sizeable aquarium, using a number of small tanks instead of one large one has several advantages. It prevents the spread of disease and enables you to separate incompatible species of fish. With smaller tanks it is possible, for example, to regulate the environment of each species individually, and to keep both salt and freshwater fish.

To support the weight of hundreds of litres of water, an aquarium cabinet like the one shown below must be much stronger than an ordinary built-in, and the floor beneath the cabinet must be strong enough to bear this weight.

If you plan to build an aquarium on a floor supported by joists, it is advisable not to have one with more than a 200-litre capacity—the same as a full bath—placed in the centre of the room. Larger aquariums must be placed against a load-bearing wall or on a floor surface over a concrete slab. Check with your aquarium supplier if you are in any doubt.

Although technically it is feasible to build your own tanks, manufactured tanks are much less prone to leaks or ruptures—and the damage that even a small leak can do to floors, ceilings and fish can be catastrophic. The tanks are available at pet shops and aquarium specialist shops, in stock sizes and to order in a rectangular shape that allows the necessary oxygen exchange at the top of the tank and an adequate swimming area for the fish. For best visibility, select a tank glued along the corners with transparent silicone rubber and framed with angle brackets along the top and bottom edges only.

In a room with limited floor space, you can build an aquarium along a wall or in an alcove. However, if you have sufficient space, the most striking location for a built-in aquarium is in the centre of the room, as a room divider.

Design the upper and lower cabinet sections so that the tank appears to float between them, at eye level, forming one continuous unit. To achieve this effect, suspend the upper cabinet (best made of exterior-grade plywood) from the ceiling, and build both cabinets almost flush with the sides of the tank, allowing them to overlap the tank slightly. Choose an inconspicuous filter system consisting of a pump hidden in the upper cabinet and a plastic tray placed on the bottom of the tank and covered with gravel.

For lighting, you can install inexpensive fluorescent aquarium fixtures in the bottomless upper cabinet. Electricity for the lights and filtration equipment can be brought into the upper cabinet from the ceiling or floor or, if it is against a wall, from the wall behind.

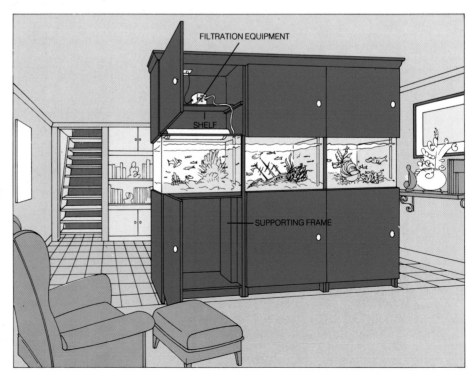

An aquarium room. This trio of floor-to-ceiling cabinets intersected by a row of glass tanks actually functions as a single unit, turning one end of a basement family room into an aquarium. The lower section of each cabinet houses a supporting frame for the tank's great weight: a wall-like internal structure of 225 by 50s and plywood, which may be fitted with shelves for storing nets, thermometers and other aquarium accessories. The frame is sheathed with a back, sides and a door of 18 mm plywood. The upper section of the cabinet, which is attached to the ceiling, is designed to allow easy access to the top of the tank for cleaning, and to provide a shelf for the filtration apparatus.

Constructing a Sturdy Aquarium Base

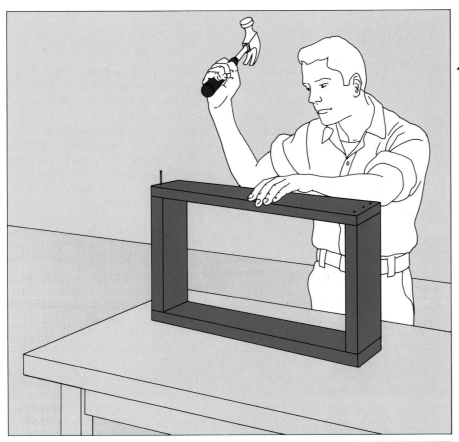

1 **Building the cabinet base.** Cut front, back and sides for the cabinet base from 100 by 50 mm timber, and assemble the base by nailing the front and back pieces to the ends of the side pieces. Make the front and back pieces 10 mm longer than the bottom of the aquarium tank; the side pieces should be 140 mm shorter than the overall width of the tank.

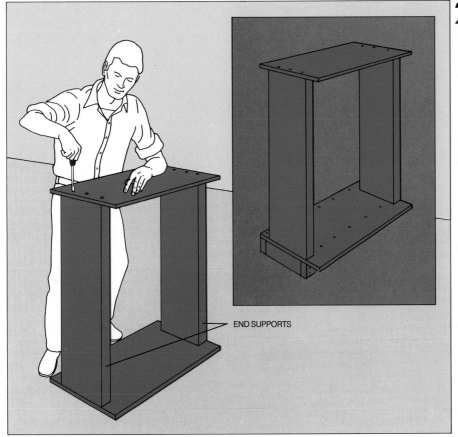

END SUPPORTS

2 **Building the supporting frame.** Assemble a frame by screwing top and bottom pieces of 18 mm plywood to 225 by 50 mm vertical supports. Cut the top and bottom pieces 10 mm wider and longer than the tank bottom, and the vertical supports 130 mm shorter than the planned height of the bottom of the tank. Make enough vertical supports to provide one at each end of the frame plus additional supports at intervals no greater than 800 mm. Centre the plywood pieces on the end supports, aligning the ends of the plywood with the outer face of the supports, and secure them with countersunk 75 mm No. 10 wood screws. Fasten the other supports at regular intervals between the two ends.

Set the bottom of the supporting frame on the cabinet base, aligning the rear edges of the frame and base *(inset)*. The front frame edge should overhang the front of the base by about 75 mm. Drive 63 mm round-wire nails through the frame bottom into the front and back edges of the base at approximately 150 mm intervals.

3 **Assembling the cabinet walls.** Make a back and sides for the supporting frame from 18 mm plywood, cutting these pieces 35 mm longer than the height of the base-and-frame assembly to provide a lip round the bottom of the tank. Cut the back 18 mm wider than the back edge of the supporting frame. Cut each side piece 35 mm wider than the end of the supporting frame, then use a router and guide board or table saw *(pages 22–25)* to cut a groove down the length of each side piece. Make the groove 18 mm wide and 9 mm deep, and position it 18 mm in from the back edge of each side piece.

Position the back against the back of the frame so that it overlaps by 9 mm on each side; nail it to the back edge of the top and bottom of the frame with lost-head nails. Spread PVA glue in the grooves of the side pieces, tap them into place over the projecting edges of the back piece, and use lost-head nails to secure them to the frame and back *(inset)*.

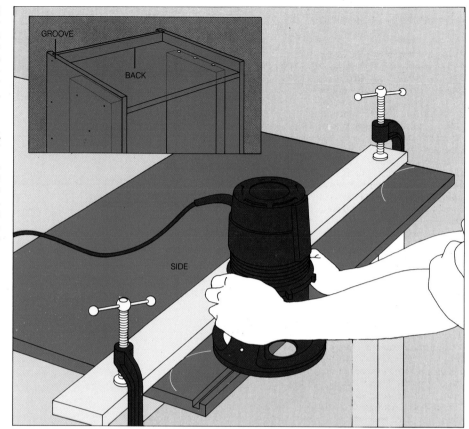

4 **Attaching the door.** Make a door of 18 mm-thick board to cover the front of the cabinet. The door should be as wide as the cabinet and high enough to reach from the bottom edge of the supporting frame to the top edge of the sides, including the top lip. The hinges should be positioned 120 mm from the top and bottom. If you are building a group of adjacent cabinets with flush doors that must open alongside each other, use concealed spring hinges that require no clearance or catch. To attach a spring hinge, outline the circular end of the hinge on the inside of the door, drill out the circle to the depth recommended by the manufacturer, and secure the round end in the hole. Screw the back plate to the cabinet side, and then screw the front plate to the back plate, adjusting the screw in the front slot so that the door fits correctly. Attach a handle.

If your cabinets will not be adjacent, you can use standard offset hinges *(inset)*. Place the flat leaves of the hinges against the inside of the door, mark their outlines with a pencil, and cut recesses as deep as the thickness of the hinge leaves, using a chisel and mallet. Screw the hinges into the recesses, hold the door against the cabinet, and outline the offset hinge leaves on the front edge and inside face of the side of the cabinet. Cut these recesses and fasten the offset leaves. Install a magnetic catch and a handle.

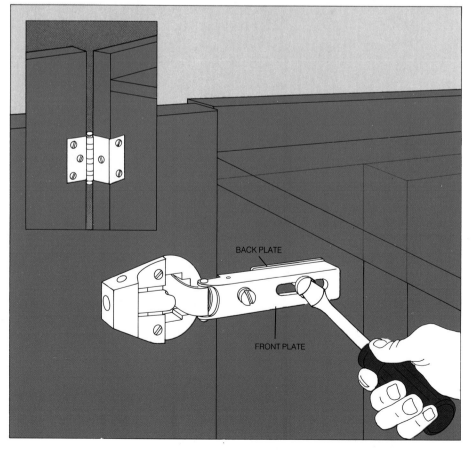

Above-the-Tank Cabinet

1 **Assembling the cabinet.** Make the sides and back for the upper cabinet the same width as those of the lower cabinet, and long enough to reach from the ceiling to a point 35 mm below the top of the tank. Make grooves in the sides and attach them to the back as in Step 3, opposite.

Cut a cabinet top to fit snugly between the sides and back, apply glue to its side and back edges; attach it with screws through the sides and back. Nail a 100 by 25 mm board across the top of the cabinet front, providing a nailing surface for coving. Cut a door and mount it *(Step 4, opposite)*. Install cleats for a shelf about 300 mm above the open bottom of the cabinet *(page 102)*, and cut a shelf to attach to the cleats after the cabinet is mounted.

To protect the upper cabinet from water vapour, use exterior-grade plywood and finish all inside surfaces with yacht varnish or polyurethane exterior varnish.

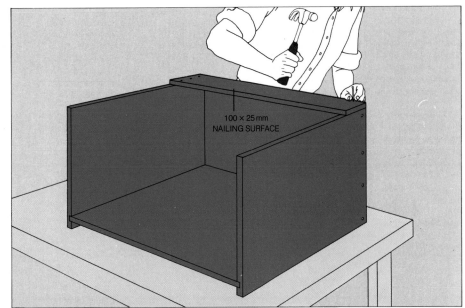

2 **Mounting the upper cabinet.** Find the positions of the ceiling joists *(page 46)*, and mark guidelines for the upper cabinet. Then get two helpers to hold the upper cabinet against the ceiling while you drill pilot holes through the plywood top and into the joists. Secure the cabinet to each joist with 75 mm No. 10 screws every 300 mm.

In concrete ceilings, drill and plug pilot holes 150 mm in from each corner of the top, and secure the cabinet with 75 mm No. 10 screws.

3 **Attaching coving.** After all the upper cabinets are in place, measure the length and width of the entire unit, and cut coving to fit, mitring the corners. Use 37 mm lost-head nails to fasten the coving to the back, side and front nailing surfaces of the cabinets, at about 300 mm intervals.

Using a plumb line, position the lower cabinets directly beneath the upper cabinets. Then open the doors and slide in the tanks.

A new bottom for a damaged drawer. The broken bottom of this drawer cannot be removed easily. It fits into grooves in the sides of the drawer, and the drawer back, which also holds the bottom in place, is fitted to the sides with intricate tongue and groove and housing joints. As the first step in a repair, the bottom must be cut into pieces and removed; a new bottom is simply installed with cleats and the thin wire nails called brads.

Many houses have built-ins—cabinets, shelves, tables, benches—and in time these built-ins may break, wear out or fail to meet new needs. But you need not go to the effort and expense of making new ones if you can repair and remodel the old. Renovating the furniture shown in Chapter 2 is a straightforward job—the parts fit together as they would in a piece built from scratch, and you need only replace them. Cabinets, however, with their drawers, doors and different methods of construction, often present special difficulties.

Newer cabinets are often constructed with "knock-down" fittings such as the jointing blocks used to assemble the shelves in Chapter 1. Taking apart such cabinets is a straightforward job; the sections are simply "knocked-down" or unscrewed, and the necessary repairs made. Older cabinets may be harder to tackle: some may follow the designs of the cabinets illustrated in Chapter 1, and be assembled with housing and rebate joints; others may be nailed or screwed to the walls piece by piece and held together by an assortment of butt joints and cleats. Many of the units may have had drawers and doors added to them in a variety of unconventional ways as the need for them arose.

Some old cabinets can be renovated with conventional woodworking tricks—worn screwholes are tightened with matchsticks and glue, doors are planed to fit, loose glue joints refastened. But often these expedients are inadequate. For one thing, they cannot remedy faults in the original construction of the cabinet—shelves made too long and now visibly sagging, or a badly constructed door that has warped. A damaged part—a scorched section of worktop, for example—may be impossible to replace invisibly. The solutions to such problems are not subtle: the shelf must be propped up with an extra partition, the door pulled straight with a stiff hardwood strip, the scorched section routed out or cut away entirely and replaced with a contrasting material. Such repairs should not be hidden; indeed, they may look worse if you attempt to conceal them. The only way to keep them from becoming eyesores is to do a neat, workmanlike job and let the repair speak for itself.

With very old cabinets, the major problem may be the design itself. Kitchen cabinets with odd-sized drawers and no partitions or floor at all make no provision for modern cooking utensils and appliances. Many old bookcases have shelves too shallow for stereo equipment and too closely spaced for large books. The only solution is to gut the cabinet interior and remodel it—substituting drawers for shelves (or vice versa), for example, or adding space-saving features of modern cabinets.

Why Cabinets Break—and How to Fix Them

Sooner or later, the strains of age and use will damage even the sturdiest built-in. For the furniture and most of the built-ins described in Chapter 2 and 3, repairs are fairly straightforward: a broken part is replaced or an entire piece is reassembled by the same method that was used to build it.

Cabinets, with their moving parts and special points of stress, are another matter. Doors warp; shelves sag; drawer bottoms crack; surfaces are damaged; and an entire cabinet frame may be forced out of true or twisted out of shape. These ills are like ailments of a body, calling for exact diagnoses and specific remedies.

The first step in diagnosis is to determine the type of cabinets you have. Some cabinets, like those in Chapter 1, may be prefabricated and secured to the wall with hanging rails; others may be suspended from the wall by interlocking cleats or special metal fittings. Some houses have backless cabinets, built by nailing cleats to a wall, then nailing shelves, sides and a frame to the cleats. In some cases, when there is no face frame, the doors are attached directly to the cabinet sides. A prefabricated cabinet is generally repaired as a unit, a backless cabinet piece by piece.

Next, determine the problem. Sagging out of level is the most common, but cabinets can also twist out of square. You can best repair a sagging prefabricated cabinet by removing it from the wall and reinstalling it *(below and opposite page, Steps 1–2; pages 46–51)*. You may be able to repair a sagging backless cabinet by pushing it against the wall and renailing its parts into place. If the sag is caused by a settling or deformed wall, the cabinet must be taken apart and reassembled on the wall *(opposite page, Steps 1–2)*.

To diagnose a cabinet that has twisted away from the wall, check the joints. If they are square and in good condition, insert shims between the cabinet and the wall to push the cabinet back into square *(page 47, Step 2)*. Joints that have popped loose must be reglued, a remedy that calls for removing the cabinet from the wall.

Like the cabinets holding them, shelves can sag from overloading. An adjustable shelf can simply be flipped over—a "repair" that can be repeated almost endlessly. Permanently fastened shelves should be permanently bolstered with supporting partitions *(below, left)*.

A support for a sagging shelf. At an end of the cabinet or bookcase, measure the distance from the bottom of the sagging shelf to the top of the shelf below. Cut a 19 mm board, of the same material as the shelf unit, as deep as the shelf and as long as the measured distance. Force this partition under the sag, then butt-nail it in place through the sagging shelf and toenail it to the shelf below.

If the lower shelf is also the bottom of the cabinet, it will support the partition permanently. If it is not, it will eventually sag below the partition; install additional partitions, working downwards, until you reach the cabinet bottom.

Squaring a Twisted Cabinet

1 **Straightening the cabinet.** Detach the cabinet from the wall by removing the screws in the hanging rail, then apply glue to any joints that have popped open—if the joints have not opened enough to admit glue, tap them open with a hammer and wood block. Close the joints with two sash cramps, set near the ends of the top and bottom rail *(below)*. Check the squareness of the cabinet by measuring diagonally across opposite corners *(page 27, Step 3)*; if the measurements are not equal, loosen the cramps, gently push one corner of the cabinet inwards until the measurements are equal, and then retighten the cramps.

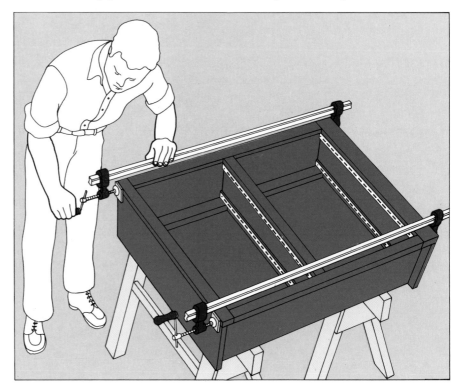

2 **Strengthening the cabinet.** Screw metal angle brackets to the joints between the top and the sides, 25 mm from the front and back of the cabinet. To strengthen the bottom joints, cut 25 by 25 mm blocks as long as the cabinet depth. At each joint, spread glue on two adjacent sides of a block, set the glued sides along the joint of the bottom and a side, and then fasten it with five 32 mm No. 6 screws, driving three screws into the bottom and two into the side.

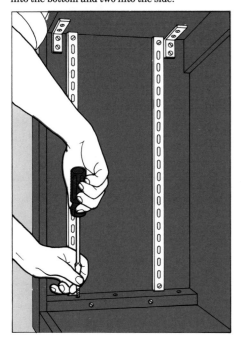

Rehanging a Backless Cabinet

1 **Taking the cabinet apart.** Remove the doors. Place a wood block against the inside of the face frame and tap it with a hammer right round the frame to loosen the joints. Grip the frame and pull it away from the shelves and sides—the nails will come out with the frame. Remove the sides and shelves in the same way, but leave the cleats beneath the shelves *(inset)* on the wall.

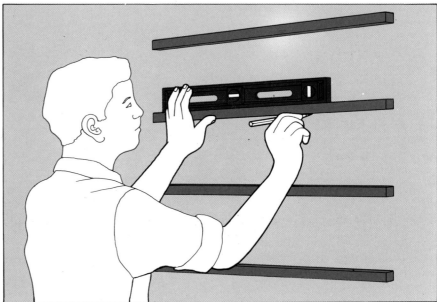

2 **Straightening the cleats.** Use a nail bar or a pair of pincers to remove some of the nails or screws that fasten each sagging cleat to the wall, leaving the nail at the high end of a cleat in place. Push the sagging end of the cleat upwards, using a level to check its position; when the cleat is level, trace its bottom edge on the wall for reference. Refasten the cleat with nails or plugged screws driven well below existing nail holes, so that the new fasteners will not slip into the old holes. Reassemble in reverse order—shelves, then sides and finally face frame.

Repairing the Moving Parts

When cabinet doors and drawers stick shut or will not close, check for small problems first. The trouble in a sticking drawer may be nothing more serious than a loose nail rubbing against a guide; if this is the case, hammer the nail back into place. A door may have a loose hinge, easily repaired by tightening the screws; if you find that the screws do not grip the wood of the door and face frame, plug the screwholes with wooden matchsticks driven into the holes and bound together with glue.

A major warp in an old solid timber door may be visible to the eye; the correct remedy is a strong hardwood brace *(right, below)*. If you suspect a minor warp in a sticking door or drawer but cannot see one, use a cabinet-maker's trick to make it visible. Run a piece of chalk along the suspected edge or guide, then close the door or drawer several times. The chalk will rub on to the cabinet and indicate the areas that need to be planed away.

A deformation of the frame is more serious. Check the cabinet in each direction with a level and by measuring the diagonals from corner to corner *(page 27, Step 3)*. If the cabinet has sagged or is twisted, you will probably have to remove and resquare it *(pages 114–115)*.

Drawers are most likely to break down at certain points of particular strain—bottoms, backstops and guides. Do not attempt to repair a bottom that has cracked or warped: it is best to remove the back of the drawer and slide a new bottom into the grooves of the drawer sides. If the grooves themselves are also damaged, install a set of cleats over the grooves for the new bottom to rest upon.

After thousands of bumps from the back of a closing drawer, backstops are eventually pushed out of place or dislodged completely: replace or thicken them with pieces of new wood. Wooden guides at the bottom of a drawer can be replaced with modern metal hardware; along the sides you must duplicate the old guides, because the metal type need more room at the sides of a drawer than the cabinet provides.

After repairing or replacing any moving part of a cabinet, prolong its life by rubbing candlewax on every edge or surface that slides upon another.

Two Ways to Fix a Deformed Door

Planing an edge. Remove the door from the cabinet and, on the inner side, mark a line 3 mm from the edge that rubs or from high spots that have been marked by chalk; secure the door in a vice. On a lipped door, as in this example, use a shoulder plane or block plane to bevel the inside edge down to the marked line. On a flush door, use a block plane, taking special care not to plane the part of the bevel near the outside edge—if you shave any wood from that edge, you will widen the critical gap between the closed door and the front frame of the cabinet.

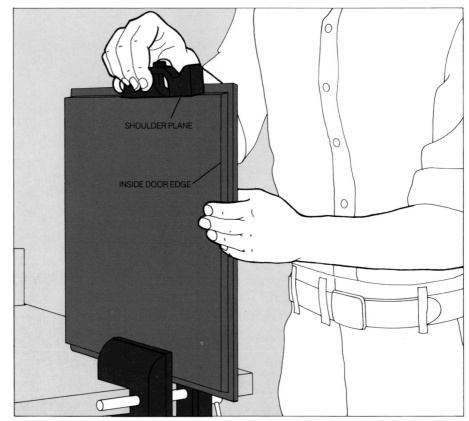

SHOULDER PLANE

INSIDE DOOR EDGE

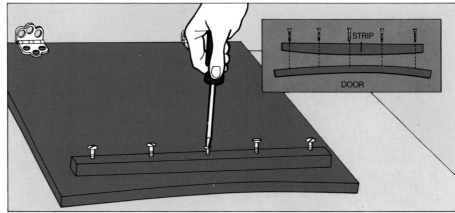

STRIP

DOOR

Bracing a warped door. Cut a strip of hardwood 50 mm shorter than the warped edge of the door, set the door face down and centre the strip 25 mm in from the warped edge. At 150 mm intervals, drive and countersink 37 mm No. 6 screws through the strip into the door. If this removes the warp, unfasten the strip, glue it in place and refasten it.

If the strip does not work, remove it and use a block plane to give it a curve opposite to the curve of the warp. Reattach the strip with the opposite curves facing each other *(inset)*. If necessary, deepen the curve of the strip repeatedly until the warp is eliminated. For a severe warp, soak the door for a few hours and tighten the screws gradually so that you do not crack the door.

Simple Cures for Ailing Drawers

Supporting a new bottom. If the sides of a drawer are cracked, or if you cannot easily remove the back to slide in a new bottom (in this example, dovetail joints make the back very difficult to remove), use cleats to support a new bottom dropped in from above. Cut two cleats about 10 mm wide, 10 mm thick and as long as each drawer side and screw them to the sides, with the tops of the cleats just above the groove tops. Apply glue to the cleat tops and use panel pins to 6 mm plywood bottom to the cleats.

CLEAT

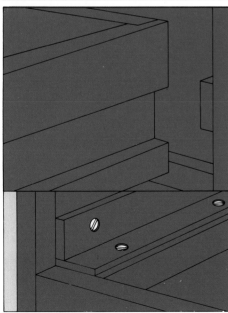

Replacing wooden side guides. In the top drawing, a drawer side is grooved to fit a cleat on a cabinet side or partition; in the bottom one, two cleats form a guide for a drawer to slide in. To replace guides, trace their outlines and remove them. Cut duplicate pieces and glue and screw them at the traced positions.

New stops on flush drawers. Remove the worn or damaged stop blocks, push the drawer in as far as it will go and measure the distance from the cabinet front to the drawer front. Cut two blocks, 25 mm square and slightly thinner than the measured distance, and tape them to the back of

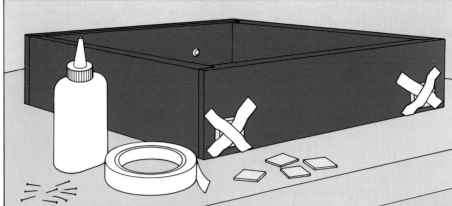

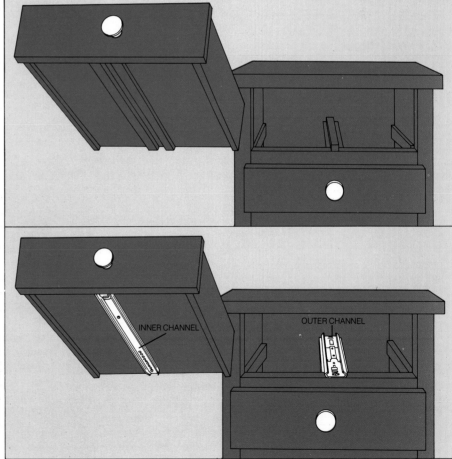

INNER CHANNEL

OUTER CHANNEL

Replacing wooden bottom guides. A wooden centre cleat, like the one in the top drawing, can be replaced by a home-made duplicate, but most professional carpenters prefer metal centre guides, which come in sizes to fit most drawers. Remove the wooden guides, measure the drawer depth and buy a centre guide to match it.

the drawer. Test the drawer in its opening and, if necessary, insert cardboard shims between the drawer back and the wood blocks until the drawer front fits flush with the cabinet front, then fasten the stops and shims permanently with glue and panel pins.

Draw a centre line down the drawer bottom and the drawer support below, if there is one—the guides will work with or without a support. Fit the inner channel to the drawer bottom and the outer channel to the cabinet, then test the drawer in its opening—if it is too low, insert cardboard shims below the outer channel.

Getting Rid of Stains, Nicks and Scorches

In a wooden surface such as a butcher's block, small dents and nicks may be acceptable or even welcome—they give the wood a certain character. In plastic laminate worktops, however, they are eyesores which can be eliminated by fillers that come in a variety of colours.

In any material, large areas of damage call for more drastic measures. Butcher's blocks must be scraped down or sanded *(opposite page, below)*. In the case of plastic laminate, the damaged section is cut out and replaced with a patch of the same material. However, it is usually difficult to remove the old section neatly, and the joins between the old and new laminate will remain visible. With certain composite worktops where the surface has been bonded to the chipboard base, it is just not possible to remove the laminate, so the whole worktop has to be replaced. An alternative is to patch the surface with a contrasting material such as ceramic tile, a wooden butcher's block, marble or granite. Before starting work, however, remember to check that the patch is not deeper than the surrounding material.

Installing an Inset of Tiles

1 **Starting the router.** Make an open, four-sided jig to the insert dimensions plus the distance between the bit and base of your router, and clamp the jig to the worktop. Set the router bit to half the depth of the tile plus 3 mm for the adhesive, tilt the router base to raise the bit above the worktop and set the base against an interior side of the jig. Turn on the router and slowly lower the bit into the worktop.

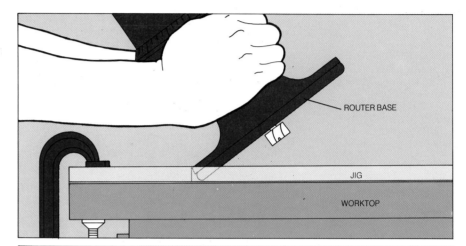

2 **Routing the inset area.** Move the router to the centre of the inset area. Working clockwise, rout out increasingly large concentric circles until the router base touches the jig, then follow the edges of the jig completely round the inset area. Repeat the process with the bit set at the full depth of the tiles plus 3 mm for the adhesive.

To square the corners, use a smaller router bit or a sharp chisel. At each corner, shift the jig outwards and use the small bit to carve corners that match your tiles.

3 **Laying the tiles.** Apply a 3 mm-thick bed of adhesive to the routed area, then set the tiles on the adhesive and let the adhesive harden for 24 hours. Fill all the joints in the tiled area with grout or silicone caulking.

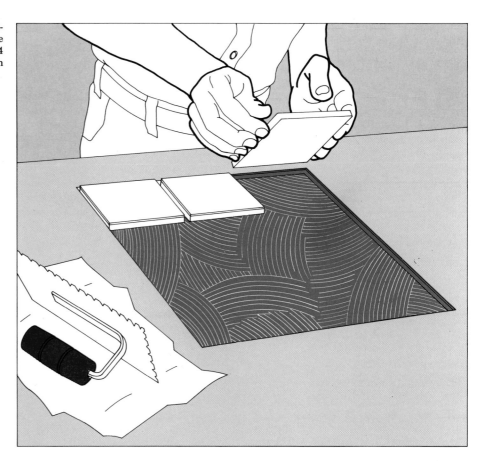

Restoring a Blemished Butcher's Block

Scraping the damage. Set the edge of a cabinet scraper, available in hardware shops, against the butcher's block at an angle of about 60 degrees and, applying even pressure, pull the scraper over the blemished area. If, after about 10 strokes, the blemish is not removed by the scraper, run a belt sander over the area—be careful not to hold the sander in one spot long enough to make a depression in the surface.

Reorganizing Inside Space for Efficiency

A built-in cabinet with a door and deep shelves makes a poor container for small, flat objects, and a cabinet with drawers is unsuitable for storing china. But if your cabinets do not match your present needs, you need not build new units; with simple carpentry and inexpensive hardware, you can substitute shelves for drawers in one cabinet (installing a partition and a bottom, if necessary), or switch from a door to drawers in another.

With even less work and trouble, you can increase the number of shelves in a unit by mounting new shelves on the back of a door, or you can add workspace with a large cutting board that slides beneath the work-top. Or you can modify your existing fittings with improvements such as slide-out shelves or vertical partitions; use exterior-grade plywood for these when cabinets are sited in steamy environments such as kitchens and bathrooms.

Before you can fashion most interior improvements, you will have to gut the cabinet. The job may be simple: to clear away doors, drawers on metal glides or shelves on metal brackets, you need only unscrew the supporting hardware. Wood mountings in old cabinets are harder to dismantle: some can be unscrewed, but most are bonded in place by old, tough glues. The mountings must be sawn into pieces, then knocked away from the cabinet walls or partitions with a hammer. Remaining nail heads must be cut off and rough places filled with wood filler. A compass saw is handy for cutting inside the confined reaches of an old cabinet. Stop sawing if the blade hits a nail or screw, and start a new cut or finish the cut with a hacksaw.

After you clear away the interior mountings, inspect the cabinet carefully. Repair loose joints and sagging or twisted units by the methods described on pages 114–115. If you plan to increase the load in a wall cabinet, reinforce its mountings with extra screws; add a hinge to a door on which you will hang shelves.

Switching from Drawers to Shelves

1 **Gutting the interior.** Remove the drawers, then cut the rails from the face frame of the cabinet as close to the sides of the openings as the fittings inside the cabinet will allow. If wooden drawer guides and supports are secured to the front and back of the cabinet, saw them in half with a compass saw *(right)* and dislodge the pieces with a hammer. To remove guides and supports that are screwed and glued to the side walls, extract the screws and tap the wood with a hammer to break the glue bonds. Cut off any remaining nails or screws with a hacksaw or snippers. Finally, cut the stub ends of the drawer rails back flush with the edges of the opening. Cover the cut edges with wood filler, allow the filler to dry, and then sand the surface smooth.

2 **Fastening cleats for a partition.** Inside a cabinet that does not have a central partition, fasten vertical 25 by 25 mm cleats to the front and back with screws and glue. To locate the back cleat, use a combination square to align a straightedge square with the front of the cabinet at the top and bottom corners of the opening *(inset)*. Mark points on the back wall directly opposite the corners. Draw a vertical line 10 mm from these marks beyond the door opening. Secure the cleat along the line; similarly mount the front cleat 10 mm away from the opening.

Cut a 9 mm-thick plywood partition for a snug fit between the front and back walls of the cabinet and tall enough to extend from the underside of the worktop to the floor.

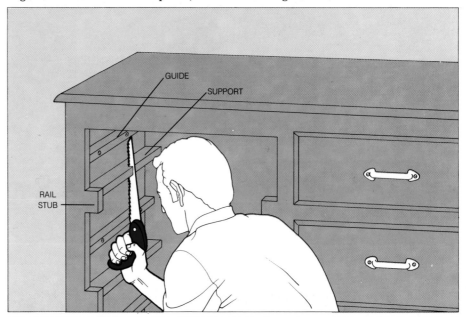

3 **Installing the partition.** In the partition, start three 25 mm panel pins, spaced evenly on a line 10 mm in from the front and back edges; spread glue on the cleats, then hold the partition against them and nail it in place. If the partition will not fit through the opening, saw it in two horizontally and mount the halves separately.

4 **Putting in a bottom.** Glue and screw a horizontal 25 by 25 mm cleat to the cabinet front, with its top edge 10 mm below the door opening. Use a level to draw similar lines on the side walls and, if it is sturdy enough to take the weight, on the back wall too. Secure cleats along the lines. Cut a 9 mm thick plywood bottom, apply glue to the top of each cleat and lay the bottom shelf on the cleats. Nail the shelf to the cleats. Finally, fit the cabinet with a door *(pages 37–41)* and install adjustable shelves *(page 11)* or other dividers.

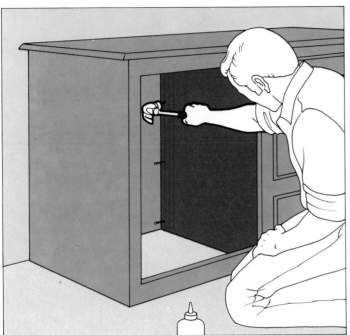

Switching from Shelves to Drawers

1 **Clearing the space.** To remove shelves glued into housings, use a jigsaw to start a V that converges at the back of the shelf, and use a compass saw to finish the cut; if the shelf extends through more than one section of the cabinet, make V cuts in each section and saw lengthwise along the middle of the shelf to connect the Vs *(right)*. Tap the top and bottom of the remaining shelf pieces with a hammer to loosen the glue, then gently work them free. If you have cut shelves that run through more than one section, install a partition between the sections *(Step 3, above)*.

To remove a shelf mounted on cleats, tap the shelf from below to break the glue bond and prise it off. Unscrew the cleats, tap them to break the glue bond and remove them. Use a hacksaw to cut off any protruding nail or screw tips.

Cut and install wood spacers for drawer glides in each drawer opening *(page 36, Step 1)*.

2 **Toenailing drawer rails.** Cut 19 mm thick timber rails to fit snugly between the drawers—use a paint scraper to clean varnish or paint from the edges of the opening where the rails will fit—and start nails at a 45-degree angle on the top and bottom of each rail, 10 mm from each end, driving the nails in until their tips just emerge from the ends *(inset)*. Apply glue to the ends of each rail, fit it in place and drive in the nails; wedging a length of scrap wood under the rail to brace it as you drive in the upper nail helps to stabilize the nailing surface. Use a nail punch to countersink the nail heads. Mount and adjust the drawer glides *(page 36, Steps 2–3)*.

Built-in Conveniences for a Built-In Cabinet

An extra working top. This pull-out cutting board is mounted between two sets of 25 by 25 mm hardwood runs, cut like cleats and spaced 1 mm wider than the thickness of the board. To begin its assembly, screw the runs to a side wall and a partition. Install a rail under the cutting board and screw a stop block to the underside of the board, 150 mm from its back edge. Screw a pull-out knob to the front edge. Trim the cabinet door so that it just overlaps the bottom edge of the rail under the cutting board. Seal the board with teak oil and rub candlewax on the side edges to help it move freely in its runs.

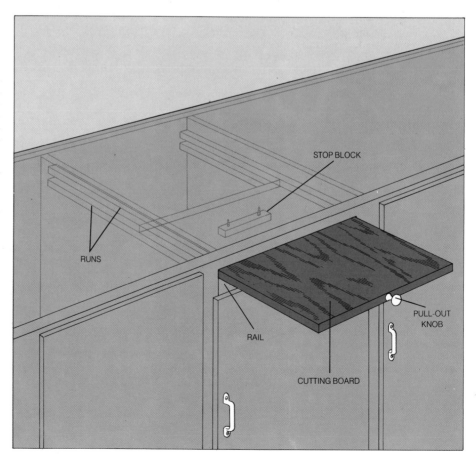

STOP BLOCK

RUNS

PULL-OUT KNOB

RAIL

CUTTING BOARD

A set of door shelves. Build the sides and shelves of this door-back unit with 9 mm plywood; use 3 mm hardboard for the back and 6 mm plywood for the edge bands, which keep objects from sliding or toppling off the shelves when the door swings. A 100 mm shelf is deep enough to hold most cans, but in planning the unit, to make sure that the shelf assembly will not block the swing of the door, tape a full-sized cardboard model of the bottom shelf to the back of the door and then close the door. Mount the unit on the door with four round-head screws; add an extra hinge to the door to support the added weight of the shelves.

If necessary, as in this example, cut back the existing shelf or shelves inside the cabinet with a jigsaw so that there will be room for the new shelves when the door is closed.

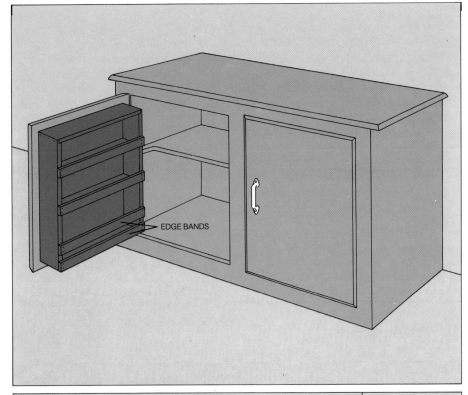

Easy access to corners. These identical quarter-round shelf units swing out for easy access when the cabinet door is opened, but rest neatly inside the cabinet when the door is closed *(inset)*. The sides and shelves are made of 9 mm plywood, the edge bands are of 6 mm plywood, and the shelf radius is 50 mm less than the width of the door opening. Attach one unit to the back of the door with screws. Mount the other on the edge of the cabinet stile, using two 75 mm butt hinges; the hinge pins should extend past the edge of the stile to allow a 180-degree swing.

If the door hinges are on the side nearer the corner, rehang the door to reverse its swing. And in the case of doors that may have to bear the weight of heavy objects, replace the existing door hinges with a piano hinge running the full height of the door, to prevent the door from dropping.

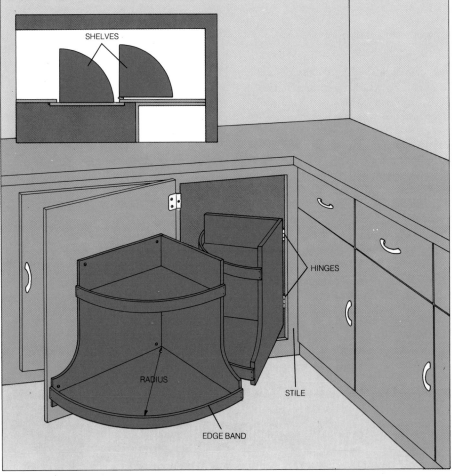

Picture Credits

The sources for the illustrations in this book are shown below. Credits for the illustrations from left to right are separated by semicolons, from top to bottom by dashes.

Cover: Fil Hunter. 6: Stephen R. Brown. 8–12: Drawings by Hayward and Martin Ltd. 13: Drawing by John Massey. 14: Drawing by John Massey—drawing by Hayward and Martin Ltd.—drawing by John Massey. 15: Drawings by John Massey. 16–21: Drawings by Ray Skibinski. 22–25: Drawings by Gerry Gallagher. 26–37: Drawings by Walter Hilmers Jr. 38: Drawing by Hayward and Martin Ltd.; drawing by Walter Hilmers Jr.—drawing by Hayward and Martin Ltd. 39: Drawings by Walter Hilmers Jr. 40: Drawing by Walter Hilmers Jr.; drawing by Hayward and Martin Ltd.; drawing by Walter Hilmers Jr.—drawings by Hayward and Martin Ltd.; drawing by Walter Hilmers Jr. 41: Drawings by Walter Hilmers Jr. 44–55: Drawings by Frederic F. Bigio from B-C Graphics. 56–60: Drawings by Ray Skibinski. 61: Drawing by Eduino Pereira. 62: Drawings by Hayward and Martin Ltd. 63–65: Drawings by Eduino Pereira. 66: Stephen R. Brown. 68–73: Drawings by Eduino Pereira. 74–83: Drawings by Frederic F. Bigio from B-C Graphics. 84–89: Drawings by John Massey. 90, 91: Drawings by Frederic F. Bigio from B-C Graphics. 92, 93: Drawings by Hayward and Martin Ltd. 94: Martin Brigdale. 96: Drawing by Hayward and Martin Ltd.— drawing by Frederic F. Bigio from B-C Graphics. 97, 98: Drawings by Frederic F. Bigio from B-C Graphics. 99: Drawing by Frederic F. Bigio from B-C Graphics— drawing by Frederic F. Bigio from B-C Graphics: drawing by Hayward and Martin Ltd. 100: Drawings by Frederic F. Bigio from B-C Graphics. 101: Drawing by James Anderson. 102: Drawing by James Anderson—drawing by Jody Ann Brown. 103: Drawings by Jody Ann Brown. 104–107: Drawings by Frederic F. Bigio from B-C Graphics. 108–111: Drawings by Snowden Associates Inc. 112: Martin Brigdale. 114–119: Drawings by Whitman Studio Inc. 120–123: Drawings by Frederic F. Bigio from B-C Graphics.

Acknowledgements

The editors would like to thank the following: Tim Fraser, Sydney; Furniture Industry Research Association, Stevenage, Herts; GKN Fasteners, Wednesbury, West Midlands; National Bedding Federation Limited, London; Nerva Metals Limited, Wembley, Middlesex; Vicki Robinson, London; Stanley Tools, Sheffield.

Index/Glossary

Metric Conversion Chart

Approximate equivalents—length

Millimetres to inches		Inches to millimetres	
1	$\frac{1}{32}$	$\frac{1}{32}$	1
2	$\frac{1}{16}$	$\frac{1}{16}$	2
3	$\frac{1}{8}$	$\frac{1}{8}$	3
4	$\frac{5}{32}$	$\frac{3}{16}$	5
5	$\frac{3}{16}$	$\frac{1}{4}$	6
6	$\frac{1}{4}$	$\frac{5}{16}$	8
7	$\frac{9}{32}$	$\frac{3}{8}$	10
8	$\frac{5}{16}$	$\frac{7}{16}$	11
9	$\frac{11}{32}$	$\frac{1}{2}$	13
10 (1cm)	$\frac{3}{8}$	$\frac{9}{16}$	14
11	$\frac{7}{16}$	$\frac{5}{8}$	16
12	$\frac{15}{32}$	$\frac{11}{16}$	17
13	$\frac{1}{2}$	$\frac{3}{4}$	19
14	$\frac{9}{16}$	$\frac{13}{16}$	21
15	$\frac{19}{32}$	$\frac{7}{8}$	22
16	$\frac{5}{8}$	$\frac{15}{16}$	24
17	$\frac{11}{16}$	1	25
18	$\frac{23}{32}$	2	51
19	$\frac{3}{4}$	3	76
20	$\frac{25}{32}$	4	102
25	1	5	127
30	$1\frac{3}{16}$	6	152
40	$1\frac{9}{16}$	7	178
50	$1\frac{31}{32}$	8	203
60	$2\frac{3}{8}$	9	229
70	$2\frac{3}{4}$	10	254
80	$3\frac{5}{32}$	11	279
90	$3\frac{9}{16}$	12 (1ft)	305
100	$3\frac{15}{16}$	13	330
200	$7\frac{7}{8}$	14	356
300	$11\frac{13}{16}$	15	381
400	$15\frac{3}{4}$	16	406
500	$19\frac{11}{16}$	17	432
600	$23\frac{5}{8}$	18	457
700	$27\frac{9}{16}$	19	483
800	$31\frac{1}{2}$	20	508
900	$35\frac{7}{16}$	24 (2ft)	610
1000 (1m)	$39\frac{3}{8}$		

Metres to feet/inches		Yards to metres	
		1	0.914
2	6′ 7″	2	1.83
3	9′ 10″	3	2.74
4	13′ 1″	4	3.66
5	16′ 5″	5	4.57
6	19′ 8″	6	5.49
7	23′ 0″	7	6.40
8	26′ 3″	8	7.32
9	29′ 6″	9	8.23
10	32′ 10″	10	9.14
20	65′ 7″	20	18.29
50	164′ 0″	50	45.72
100	328′ 1″	100	91.44

Conversion factors

Length

1 millimetre (mm)	= 0.0394 in
1 centimetre (cm)/10 mm	= 0.3937 in
1 metre/100 cm	= 39.37 in/3.281 ft/1.094 yd
1 kilometre (km)/1000 metres	= 1093.6 yd/0.6214 mile
1 inch (in)	= 25.4 mm/2.54 cm
1 foot (ft)/12 in	= 304.8 mm/30.48 cm/0.3048 metre
1 yard (yd)/3 ft	= 914.4 mm/91.44 cm/0.9144 metre
1 mile/1760 yd	= 1609.344 metres/1.609 km

Area

1 square centimetre (sq cm)/ 100 square millimetres (sq mm)	= 0.155 sq in
1 square metre (sq metre)/10,000 sq cm	= 10.764 sq ft/1.196 sq yd
1 are/100 sq metres	= 119.60 sq yd/0.0247 acre
1 hectare (ha)/100 ares	= 2.471 acres/0.00386 sq mile
1 square inch (sq in)	= 645.16 sq mm/6.4516 sq cm
1 square foot (sq ft)/144 sq in	= 929.03 sq cm
1 square yard (sq yd)/9 sq ft	= 8361.3 sq cm/0.8361 sq metre
1 acre/4840 sq yd	= 4046.9 sq metres/0.4047 ha
1 square mile/640 acres	= 259 ha/2.59 sq km

Volume

1 cubic centimetre (cu cm)/ 1000 cubic millimetres (cu mm)	= 0.0610 cu in
1 cubic decimetre (cu dm)/1000 cu cm	= 61.024 cu in/0.0353 cu ft
1 cubic metre/1000 cu dm	= 35.3147 cu ft/1.308 cu yd
1 cu cm	= 1 millilitre (ml)
1 cu dm	= 1 litre see **Capacity**
1 cubic inch (cu in)	= 16.3871 cu cm
1 cubic foot (cu ft)/1728 cu in	= 28,316.8 cu cm/0·0283 cu metre
1 cubic yard (cu yd)/27 cu ft	= 0.7646 cu metre

Capacity

1 litre	= 1.7598 pt/0.8799 qt/0.22 gal
1 pint (pt)	= 0.568 litre
1 quart (qt)	= 1.137 litres
1 gallon (gal)	= 4.546 litres

Weight

1 gram (g)	= 0.035 oz
1 kilogram (kg)/1000 g	= 2.20 lb/35.2 oz
1 tonne/1000 kg	= 2204.6 lb/0.9842 ton
1 ounce (oz)	= 28.35 g
1 pound (lb)	= 0.4536 kg
1 ton	= 1016 kg

Pressure

1 gram per square metre ($g/metre^2$)	= 0.0295 oz/sq yd
1 gram per square centimetre (g/cm^2)	= 0.228 oz/sq in
1 kilogram per square centimetre (kg/cm^2)	= 14.223 lb/sq in
1 kilogram per square metre ($kg/metre^2$)	= 0.205 lb/sq ft
1 pound per square foot (lb/ft^2)	= 4.882 $kg/metre^2$
1 pound per square inch (lb/in^2)	= 703.07 $kg/metre^2$
1 ounce per square yard (oz/yd^2)	= 33.91 $g/metre^2$
1 ounce per square foot (oz/ft^2)	= 305.15 $g/metre^2$

Temperature

To convert °F to °C, subtract 32, then divide by 9 and multiply by 5
To convert °C to °F, divide by 5 and multiply by 9, then add 32

Phototypeset by Tradespools Limited, Frome, Somerset
Colour reproduction by Grafascan Limited
Printed and bound by Artes Gráficas, Toledo, SA, Spain

D. L. TO: 1230 -1985 X